HOW TO
WORK
WITH
THE MEDIA

9/00

SURVIVAL SKILLS FOR SCHOLARS

Managing Editor: Mitchell Allen

Survival Skills for Scholars provides you, the professor or advanced graduate student working in a college or university setting, with practical suggestions for making the most of your academic career. These brief, readable guides will help you with skills that you are required to master as a college professor but may have never been taught in graduate school. Using hands-on, jargon-free advice and examples, forms, lists, and suggestions for additional resources, experts on different aspects of academic life give invaluable tips on managing the day-to-day tasks of academia—effectively and efficiently.

Volumes in This Series

SURVIVAL SKILLS FOR SCHOLARS

HOW TO WORK WITH THE MEDIA

JAMES ALAN FOX

JACK LEVIN

SAGE Publications
International Educational and Professional Publisher
Newbury Park   London   New Delhi

For information address:

 SAGE Publications, Inc.
2455 Teller Road
Newbury Park, California 91320

SAGE Publications Ltd.
6 Bonhill Street
London EC2A 4PU
United Kingdom

SAGE Publications India Pvt. Ltd.
M-32 Market
Greater Kailash I
New Delhi 110 048 India

Printed in the United States of America

Library of Congress Cataloging-in-Publication Data

Fox, James Alan.
  How to work with the media / James Alan Fox, Jack Levin.
      p.   cm. — (Survival skills for scholars ; vol. 2)
  ISBN 0-8039-5088-8 (cl.). — ISBN 0-8039-5089-6 (pbk.)
  1. Mass media and educators—United States. 2. Public relations—
Universities and colleges—United States. I. Levin, Jack, 1941-.
II. Title. III. Series.
LB2342.8.F69 1993
659.2'937878—dc20   93-24841

93 94 95 96 10 9 8 7 6 5 4 3 2 1

Sage Production Editor: Judith L. Hunter

Contents

Acknowledgments*

W e are pleased to recognize several individuals who helped us through various stages of this project. Most important, our editor, Mitch Allen, was a constant source of guidance from start to finish. We also benefited from the insightful comments of two anonymous reviewers. Also, Kim Gorniak skillfully tracked down various data that we were lacking.

We are grateful to a number of individuals who, over the years, have encouraged and assisted us in attracting favorable publicity and avoiding "bad press." Northeastern University has maintained a strong public relations office from whose staff we have benefited considerably. In particular, we have enjoyed working with the following public relations specialists, "in order of appearance": Chris Mosher, James King, Joan Koffman, Paul Jones, Tom Estes, Charles Coffin, Joanne Legg, Terry Yanulavich, Janet Hookalow, and Mary Breslauer. We also appreciate the support of Northeastern University President John A. Curry, Provost Michael A. Baer, and Dean Robert Lowndes. In addition, we thank our wives and children for their patience waiting for us to get off the phone, and members of our office staffs—including Shirley Davis, Marilyn Kearney, Marilyn Churchill, George Bradt,

* Fox and Levin contributed equally to this work; the listing of authorship was determined by alphabetical order alone.

Monica Cantwell, and Kitty Walsh—for taking extraordinary efforts to locate us when the media call. Finally, we owe a special debt of gratitude to our answering machines, without "whose" help we would have a lot more time to do other things.

JAMES ALAN FOX

JACK LEVIN

1 | Deciding to Go Public

Have you ever thought of trying to justify your career to John Q. Taxpayer? John Q. knows that you teach his kids; but other than that, he thinks that you're sitting there in your office, staring out the window, thinking great thoughts, and collecting a paycheck for teaching 6 hours a week—except when you're ripping him off by using taxpayer money to study sexual imagery in porno magazines. Showing off your knowledge and hard work on the *Evening News* can provide some important benefits to you, your department, your school, your discipline, and even academia itself. In the wake of Senator William Proxmire's "Golden Fleece Awards" for apparently frivolous research and more recent scandals about the misappropriation of grant funds, universities could certainly use some good press.

This guide is designed to assist academics in making the most of their encounters with the media, be they regular or occasional. Whether you actively seek publicity for your work or just want to be prepared when a reporter calls for an insightful comment, we hope the advice we offer will make your media experiences more enjoyable and more productive.

As strong advocates of proactive media relations, we understand, nonetheless, that there are advantages and disadvantages to these activities. It is our objective to help you maximize the positive and minimize the negative, at least to the extent possible. In the chapters to follow, we examine the role of academics in television, radio, newspapers, and magazines, giving pointers and case studies from our own experiences. We also present Q&A interviews with representatives of the mass media for their perspective regarding the relationship of academics to the media.

If only to establish our credibility in preparing this book, we should say up front that we have probably appeared on thousands of television and radio programs and have given a similar number of interviews to newspaper reporters. Admittedly, one of the many things that we have learned from these experiences is why so many of our colleagues in academia literally run from the press and talk-show interviewers. There really are tremendous costs involved with the media, mostly in terms of wasted time.

We definitely get mixed reactions from our colleagues. Many, if not most, of them encourage and support our media activities. Some are proud to identify with the school or discipline being publicized. A few, however, see our activities as outside (and even beneath) the role appropriate for serious academics.

We don't do it for the money. It might come as a surprise that the national shows (such as *Good Morning America* and *Geraldo*) generally pay only for travel expenses. Of course, there was the time when the producer of a major talk show, as a last resort, offered one of us money to miss an important faculty meeting and fly to a taping in New York City instead. As tempting as it was, the offer was refused.

Sometimes a local program in a distant city may pay a fee, but hardly enough to compensate for the extensive amount of time involved. A couple hundred dollars hardly pays for the inconvenience of flying 12 hours coast-to-coast (unless you make a mini-vacation of it). There are exceptions here, too. For example, a Detroit television station asked one of us to do an interview from Boston by satellite. Because it was Friday evening and a major infringement on family plans, the station was willing to pay for a limousine and dinner for two at any

Boston restaurant. We're not for sale, of course, but did someone mention food?

Having chosen an academic career in the first place, money is hardly our primary incentive in life (although we do not dislike it either). There are other kinds of payoffs, however, which may not pay the bills but are valuable nonetheless. After all, how else would we have met the mother of the infamous "Hillside Strangler," the man who lost 350 pounds by stapling his stomach; or stars from *Days of Our Lives* (Jack's favorite show) and professional sports (which Jamie prefers). As you will see, there are many other professional rewards and fringe benefits, which, on balance, make media involvement a worthwhile pursuit.

The Good News

Over the years, both of us have, on occasion, had to justify our intensive media involvement to skeptical colleagues (not to mention our spouses). Some academics feel strongly that appearing on television is a complete waste of time—that it is far preferable to spend the time toiling in the laboratory or writing journal articles instead. In the academic world, we are constantly making choices about how to spend our time— whether to work on our lecture notes, attend a certain convention, or hit the word processor. In almost everything we do, our goal is to disseminate our ideas—to students in a class, to colleagues at a seminar, or to readers of a professional journal.

Another important constituency for academic research and knowledge too often overlooked by traditional academics in many fields includes policymakers, community leaders, and average citizens. No one but your colleagues, an occasional student, and your mother will read your research findings if only published in a professional journal or monograph. Expanding your ideas outside the walls of academia will maximize the impact of your work and will, in the process, more widely legitimate your efforts.

For example, researchers in criminology have important information to share regarding the disutility of the death penalty. Yet, some scholars never address an audience beyond the colleagues in their field. They may write important articles in academic journals, read pioneering papers at professional meetings, and share valuable data with other criminologists, and yet fail to make full use of the most powerful means for influencing public opinion—the mass media. We are suggesting that academics be not only responsive to the media, but proactive as well. In certain topics of vital concern, it may be our duty.

In this book, we advocate that academics broaden their audience—to bridge the cultures of academia and everyday society. Our approach relies heavily on presentation of self. However, this should not be misinterpreted as a substitute for solid academic research as the foundation for generating and testing ideas. Furthermore, we view the mass media as complementary to traditional academic means for disseminating information, not as a substitute.

In our years of experience with the media, we have enjoyed many advantages. These are available to academics who are willing to invest the time in "working" the media. As in all academic choices involving the allocation of time and energy, one must consider whether the benefits outweigh the costs. The benefits reaped from media involvement vary, of course, by the type of participation, and also by your own particular situation. For example, untenured assistant professors must assess the attitudes and expectations of their senior colleagues as well as formal requirements for tenure in determining how much time they wish to spend with the press. In addition, all faculty might consider the outlook of their college or university toward publicity. At one extreme, your school, particularly if it depends largely on tuition revenue for its operating budget, should appreciate the public relations value of high-profile faculty. At the other extreme, your school might take the position that media exposure actually diminishes the prestige of the faculty. Most schools are in between, and maintain the view that media participation is a reasonably important activity for its faculty when it doesn't interfere with classes (except, of course, if the class itself is being filmed for television).

Consistent with a balanced view, we should highlight both the positive and negative consequences of dealing with the media. Reflecting our position that the advantages tend to outweigh the disadvantages, however, we nonarbitrarily choose to start with the benefits.

- *Influence.* It's like speaking to a classroom of millions, or like teaching a very large service course, "Introduction to Whatever," to nonmajors. In this way, it is like most undergraduate teaching—designed for the purpose of producing educated, well-rounded people, not for training students to be researchers or scholars. Not only can you enlighten the general public, but you may also persuade public officials and influence policymakers who might otherwise be unaware of important research.

  In addition, there is something especially gratifying about speaking to a "classroom" of viewers who tune in just because they are interested in hearing what you have to say, not because they have to do well on the final exam. Finally, the skills required to become a competent media expert—speaking clearly and succinctly in an interesting fashion—in turn fine-tune one's effectiveness as a classroom lecturer.

- *Status.* Publicity tends to elevate your stature, credibility, and value with students and their parents, alumni, and prospective students. Most students are impressed when they see their professors on television. Not only does it strengthen the students' school pride, but it also enhances your credibility in their eyes. Even though this may not be an appropriate or fair standard of assessing academic reputation, to most undergraduates one appearance on *The Oprah Winfrey Show* is worth a thousand journal articles.

Parents are even more impressed. Seeing their child's professor on national television convinces them that they must be getting their money's worth—after all, they can rest assured that the classes are being taught by nationally recognized experts. The value of faculty publicity is magnified in terms of the perceptions of alumni and other important constituencies who don't necessarily subscribe to academic journals, but do watch television and read the daily newspaper.

- *Recognition.* The potential for community recognition is also a nice fringe benefit. Although for some it may only serve to boost their ego, exposure in the public airwaves can have some practical advantages as well. For example, being seen as a local celebrity can open doors for someone who is interested in local governance or in speaking to community groups.

- *Professional recognition.* Although not nearly as valued as an academic citation, being quoted in the news can advance your academic stature in the eyes of at least some professional colleagues. In fact, they are probably more apt to remark to you that they saw you quoted in *The New York Times* than that they saw you cited in the *American Journal of This and That.*

In a related sense, the reputation of your academic discipline is also boosted from media exposure. For example, while some academic psychologists might wish to distance themselves from "media shrinks" such as Dr. Joyce Brothers and a number of other lesser-known on-air counselors, the professional credibility of the field of psychology has clearly benefited. In contrast, a field such as sociology, receiving far less media attention, continues to be confused with social work or even socialism by lay persons who are unfamiliar with the work of academic sociologists.

- *Additional opportunities.* Publicity can lead to opportunities for other kinds of activities. Media involvement, for example, can result in invitations to join speakers' bureaus, give keynote talks, consult for corporations or government agencies, affiliate with agents and publishers, and render expert testimony. You may even get to meet potential subjects for future research and writing.

Case Study

Shortly after the grisly discovery of the bodies of five college students in Gainesville, Florida, in August 1990, *Donahue* staged a live, on-location program from Gainesville concerning the crimes. One of the authors (Jamie) was invited to be on the panel of guests to speak about serial murder. Following the *Donahue* program, Jamie was asked by the police task force investigating the murders to provide his insights into the unsolved homicides. Eventually, this role became formalized into a consulting arrangement with the Florida Department of Law Enforcement. This provided invaluable insights and unusual access, not to mention information for future research on serial murder.

- *Tangible benefits.* The perks aren't bad, either. Television stations, syndicates, and networks typically do not pay academic experts in cash, but royal treatment certainly counts for something. Not only do the limousine service, fine restaurants and hotels, and the chance to meet interesting people provide an enjoyable change from routine academic life, but the frequent flier mileage credits will help pay for the family vacation.

The Bad News

In light of the many benefits to media involvement, why don't more academics talk to reporters and appear on air? At least some academics are elitist in their reticence, others are (sometimes justifiably) afraid of being misrepresented or misquoted, and some are just too nervous in front of a camera. Clearly, there are some real drawbacks and potential pitfalls that deter many academics from becoming media oriented.

- *Time demands.* The most prominent objection to media involvement is that it consumes (and sometimes wastes) a lot of valuable time that might otherwise be spent on more productive activities. After all, you usually don't get paid, much of what you say could get cut, and you might not even get on at all.

  For example, you can spend an hour talking with a reporter, and even researching a topic for her, and still not get mentioned in the article. She might even use your ideas, but not attribute them to you. Or, she might include your name (spelled correctly or not), but fail to identify your academic affiliation correctly. (Both of us teach at Northeastern University, but we have garnered a fair amount of publicity for Northwestern.)

  Finally, for those who choose to be proactive in publicizing their work, there is a tremendous amount of time needed to cultivate a media presence—to develop and maintain contacts and relationships with members of the media. Schmoozing with reporters and producers is very time-consuming (even if they pay for lunch), and the payoff may not come for years after the initial investment.

- *Disruption.* The media can be very disruptive to your work and home life. It is never on your schedule; it is always on theirs. Opportunities for publicity don't occur with the regularity that your teaching does. You must be ready and willing to cooperate when *they* need you, whether it is convenient for you or not. Reporters, in order to meet a deadline, often call at the worst times—toward the end of the day when you're about to go home, when you are speaking with a student in your office, or when you are in the middle of dinner.

- *No control.* The limited time allotment may not allow you to do justice to what you have to say. Control is simply not in your hands. And once spoken, your remarks can be reduced, taken out of context, excised altogether, or even used without permission.

- *Their agenda.* You also have no control over the agenda. Although certain topics play well in the media (or at least the producers think so), other topics do not. You may feel personally involved with the issue of health care for the elderly, but the producer wants to address elder abuse. You may have done research on intervention strategies for juvenile offenders, but the producer cares only about kids who kill.

- *Peer disapproval.* Your colleagues may discount the value of your contributions to the media or may disregard them altogether. Academic departments generally do not reward media contributions in terms of merit raises, tenure, and promotion the way they do for more traditional scholarly activities. In departments that place a premium on publishing, moreover, senior colleagues may even count media involvement negatively in the evaluation process, seeing it as a distraction from academic writing and research.

On occasion, you may do an interview about some topic on which you are knowledgeable, but not the leading authority. You may run the risk of offending a colleague who considers himself or herself to be more qualified to address the topic. Keep in mind, however, that you may have been contacted for many reasons in addition to your expertise, including accessibility, previous publicity, and your ability to communicate clearly.

- *Public disapproval.* You take a chance with your ego. At the very least, even when tenure or promotion is not an issue, a few colleagues at your university as well as at other institutions may lose respect for you, characterizing you as a "media hound." You also run the risk of getting negative mail and phone calls from people who disagree with your remarks. Academic freedom will not protect you from the hate mail, death threats, and harassing calls you may receive should you advocate an unpopular point of view regarding a controversial topic.

Case Study

One of us (Jamie) tends to be outspoken in his unwavering opposition to the death penalty. Even when discussing a case involving brutal crimes against children, he maintains his abolitionist view. Although it is generally safe to express staunch opposition to capital punishment at a professional conference or in a classroom, you take a risk by arguing this position in the media. Prompted by his antideath-penalty rhetoric on television and in the press, Jamie has received vicious phone calls and letters. For example, some have gone as far as to suggest in a threatening, almost prophetic manner that "he would feel differently if his child were murdered." And one irate letter-writer wrote Jamie's superiors at the university in an effort to have him "academically executed."

Coming Up Next

Now that you are well informed about the advantages and pitfalls of working with the media, we hope that on balance you will decide to go public. If so, there are some fundamentals that you will need to consider in order to get started on the right foot.

2 | Getting Started

In the old *Mary Tyler Moore* television series, news anchor Ted Baxter frequently reminisced about having started his career as a disc jockey on an obscure 10,000-watt radio station. Ted Baxter may have been fictional, but his message was quite real. People in the media recognize that you have to "pay your dues" by starting at the bottom and working your way up the ladder of success.

What may be obligatory for most media people is sound advice for academics who seek media publicity—prepare for *Face the Nation* by first facing the local community. Gain experience on a small scale, where mistakes are forgiven, before attempting the "big-time," where nothing less than perfection is expected. Starting small provides the opportunity not only to become comfortable with the technical aspects of an unfamiliar medium, but also to build confidence in your media skills.

Most of us did not deliver our first lecture to a packed classroom of 500 freshmen. Likewise, most people with little or no television experience are ill-prepared to perform on *The Oprah Winfrey Show* in a manner that will show them in a positive light.

Starting Small

There is a wide variety of places to begin. Don't feel embarrassed about rehearsing with a tape recorder or, better yet, a camcorder. For on-air experience, you may turn to your local cable-access station, or even a campus radio station. You should also consider doing local public affairs interview shows—often aired early Sunday mornings when all your students and colleagues are still asleep. Although no one you know may see you and you're not reaching millions (or even thousands) with your message, you are benefiting nonetheless through gaining both experience and confidence.

Case Study

The two of us met in 1977 at a party in the Sociology Department at Northeastern University. Standing over the tabouli, we discovered that we had a mutual interest in talk radio, and on the spur of the moment decided to try hosting our own show. The extremely small campus radio station (it seemed to have fewer watts than a "nightlite") was more than happy to accommodate us. For almost a year we cohosted a weekly talk show, *NU Ideas*. (Jamie had to practice saying "ideas," instead of "idears," without his Boston accent.)

We probably had more fun than we had listeners. We also had the golden opportunity to work on our technique by reviewing and critiquing tapes of our on-air performance. At the beginning, Jack used to read almost every word from a prepared script; but over time, he learned to ad lib as he had always felt comfortable doing in the classroom. Jamie developed a keener sense of timing for his puns and got rid of his Boston accent as well.

Despite the inherent value of practicing on a campus station, it was certainly frustrating. It wasn't that our guests were uninteresting—on the contrary, we were fortunate to have some well-known and articulate personalities on our show. But the station's signal only spanned a five-block radius, and that was on a clear night. After 10 months we received our first and only letter from a fan.

Having polished our act, we approached a major, 50,000-watt affiliate of National Public Radio with tapes of our best shows.

Fortunately, we were given a prime half-hour time slot and were assigned a producer. For more than a year, we hosted a weekly program called *Making Waves*. We interviewed authors of books on important social issues, celebrities from sports and entertainment, and controversial community activists. Once we even interviewed a famous restauranteur over the best dinner his money could buy.

Getting Ready

Once you feel confident about seeking publicity, there are a few things you will need to prepare.

- *After initial phone contact, many producers will ask you to fax them a media resumé or bio.* This is not the same as your curriculum vitae in either length or content. Prepare a one-page overview of your accomplishments in which you provide your name with highest degree earned; title and affiliation; address; *all* phone numbers (office, home, fax, and answering machine); areas of specialization; major publications *without* academic citations; speaking engagements; and experience with television, radio, and newspapers, listed separately. (For example, see our one-page media bios included at the end of this guide.) Or, you may choose to write a brief biographical sketch containing similar information but in less detail. The latter is particularly useful for those with little media experience.

- *Newspapers (reporters, feature writers, and op-ed editors) may ask you to supply a professional photograph of yourself through overnight delivery.* Almost immediately you will need to send a copy of a black-and-white "head shot." Because this leaves insufficient time to run out to a studio to have a new picture taken and developed, you should keep several copies on file.

- *When you deal with the media, time is really of the essence.* Reporters are constantly on deadline; thus if they can't reach you quickly, then they will call someone else. Therefore you *must* have a reliable answering machine with remote capability. You also must be willing to check for messages frequently, particularly if there is a breaking news story related to your area of expertise or if you have just done an interview that might generate follow-up inquiries. Promptly return phone messages from reporters and producers. It is acceptable to return a message with a collect person-to-person call.

- *The busier you get, the busier your phone line will get.* At this point, you may not need a cellular phone or a pager, but some technology will surely help. Thus you should consider installing call-waiting or a two-line phone. You certainly don't want to be bypassed by *The New York Times* because your line is tied up by a reporter from the *Podunk Post* who keeps having "just one more question." Finally, although not essential, you should have access to a fax machine at home or the office. You may be asked to send your bio by fax, or you may use the fax machine to achieve quick and widespread submission of a time-dependent op-ed column. You may also benefit from having background material faxed to you in preparation for a telephone interview with a radio station or newspaper.

- *Don't get caught with your pants down.* We can't give you advice on what to wear, because only you know what makes you look your best. What looks great in person, however, doesn't always come across well on television. For example, small stripes appear to quiver and small prints tend to blur. Many people achieve the best results with dark, solid-colored suits accompanied by brightly colored accessaries (ties and scarves). Above all, avoid wearing stark white because it tends to give you a "washed out" look.

No matter how effective your wardrobe, it will do you little good if you don't have the right clothing with you when you need it. If you are one of the many academics who dresses informally at school, consider keeping an appropriate suit of clothes in a garment bag at the office should the *Evening News* call for a last-minute interview.

- *Learn the players and their roles.* Tables 2.1 and 2.2 provide lists of the many kinds of media personnel with whom you are likely to have contact: You should learn not only who they are but also what they do. Also, when you read the newspaper, make a mental note of the names of writers and reporters in your area of interest. When you watch a news or talk show, pay attention to the credits at the end. For your own future reference, moreover, it is helpful to keep a record of who from the media calls you and for what purpose. Create a notebook of names, numbers, and interests of reporters and producers.

Working With Public Relations

Recognizing the value of positive publicity, not just for the president but also for the faculty, more and more colleges and universities have established public relations offices. Large or small, these departments are staffed with media specialists who combine both expertise in a variety of media with a wealth of contacts. For the faculty member who is willing to learn, it's almost like having a publicity agent and a coach, without having to pay for them.

It is important to keep in touch with the specialists in your school's public relations office so that they are aware of your willingness to do interviews. In addition, make sure that they are informed of the progress of your research so that they can help to plan a media strategy. Also, apprise them of your own interactions with the media, including any newspaper articles in which you have been quoted or shows on which you

Table 2.1 Television and Radio Personnel

Title	Role
Executive Producer	You may never meet the big boss, but he pays the bills and makes the major financial decisions. (Academic equivalent = Dean)
(Senior) Producer	This person calls the shots on an everyday basis about programming for television and radio. In a small market, the producer has responsibility over virtually everything, including what topics and guests will be featured. In a large operation, the senior producer oversees a staff of associate and assistant producers. (Academic equivalent = Department Chair)
Associate Producer	These people do the everyday tasks of arranging a show and booking the guests. You will probably deal most with the associate producer, including the initial phone contact as well as a screening preinterview. (Academic equivalent = Professors/Instructors)
Talent	This generic term covers the host of a talk show, the anchor of a newscast, or even an on-air reporter. You may not get to meet this person until you are actually on the set. (Academic equivalent = Distinguished Professor)
Interns	These people are the trainees (often college students) who might arrange your travel or reimbursement, escort you around the station, and get coffee. (Academic equivalent = we wish!)
Other	Major shows divide the tasks among a number of specialized roles, including bookers (to find the guests), researchers (to collect information about a topic), and travel coordinators (to arrange for your hotel and transportation). (Academic equivalents = Assistant Deans, Administrative Assistants, Research Assistants, and Secretaries)

have appeared. Not only will this enhance your reputation in their view, but they may see that you get the credit you deserve around the university. Finally, supply them with an

Table 2.2 Newspaper and Magazine Personnel

Title	Role
Executive Editor	You will likely never encounter this person. He or she works behind the scenes, making the major editorial and publication decisions. (Academic equivalent = Dean)
Editor	This person has responsibility over a specialized portion of the publication; for example, the living, metro, sports, op-ed, education, or science section. Generally, this individual assigns reporters to cover particular events or stories. (Academic equivalent = Department Chair)
Reporters	These people do the research and write the stories. You will probably have most contact with them. (Academic equivalent = Professors/Instructors)
Staff Writers	This term includes columnists and feature writers. You may hear from them on rare occasions for a quote in a piece or even a profile. (Academic equivalent = Distinguished Professor)
Freelancers/ Stringers	This term includes writers who are commissioned to write a single story or who contribute on a regular but part-time basis. (Academic equivalent = Part-time/Adjunct Professors)
Fact Checkers	Usually employed by magazines, these people assist the editors and may call you to verify quotes, names, titles, and dates. (Academic equivalent = Teaching/Research Assistants)

up-to-date photograph and bio, in case they get calls on your behalf.

The valuable services that may be performed by in-house PR personnel include:

1. assisting in the preparation and distribution of press releases on newsworthy research that you are doing;
2. identifying appropriate media targets for publicizing your work based on their own personal contacts as well as published media directories;

3. making referrals of news reporters from television, radio, and daily papers to you in areas of your expertise;

4. preparing media kits that feature your work, containing a press release, clippings, bio, photo, and a copy of the report for which publicity is sought;

5. accompanying you to programs in order to provide support and guidance and to help you deal effectively with production staff;

6. providing you with one-on-one training in developing media skills;

7. reviewing and critiquing drafts of your op-ed columns and making inquiries to op-ed editors for you;

8. making videotapes of television appearances and collecting newsclips of your news quotes; and

9. alerting administrators on campus, including the president, your dean and chair, of how valuable a contribution to the university your publicity has been.

Being Newsworthy

Once you have the competence, confidence, accoutrements, and contacts, you then need to find the right "spin" to your topic or subject matter that will attract the attention and interest of news directors, assignment editors, reporters, and producers. Obviously, certain topics are more newsworthy than others. Any academic who studies crime, the economy, psychology, medicine, or politics will have far more opportunities than someone who studies medieval literature or pure math. Regardless of your field, however, there are ways to increase your newsworthiness.

Be creative and flexible in finding angles in your area of expertise that can apply to everyday issues and events of widespread concern. For example, a physicist might be prepared to comment on the physical laws pertaining to a major plane crash in the news, even if he or she hasn't conducted original research on this application of physics. A historian who specializes in the era of the Great Depression might have a lot of insight regarding today's economic trends, even if he or she is not trained as an economist. You can give insight and provide perspective without having conducted firsthand research. Remember, you are not talking to an audience of your peers at an academic gathering, nor are you writing for your colleagues. Ask yourself whether you can inform the general public—whether you can increase their knowledge about something they are eager to understand. Use the same approach that you take in the classroom. You can be *an* expert even if you are not *the* expert.

We must point out an important note of caution regarding our advice about being responsive to questions that may not exactly be up your alley. Just like academics, most reporters want to speak to specialists. By looking too much like a generalist—by being willing to comment on any topic related to your field, no matter how thinly connected—you risk losing your credibility.

In interviews with the mass media, it is critical to be understood. Some academics mistakenly assume that they must employ stilted language—especially jargon, obscure or multisyllabic words, and complex syntax—in order to appear smart. Even if this is not their everyday style of speech, some feel that they should sound like an expert—after all, isn't that why they were contacted? Actually, you don't have to talk down to people for them to look up to you. In the mass media, you must be understood by the masses.

This does not mean that you must abandon all terminology of your field, although using jargon without defining it in an intelligible way will make you look pompous and boring. You *can* use jargon in an effective way, however, by explaining it in an easy-to-understand context. By demystifying the specialized language of your discipline, you come across as genuine, interesting, and very intelligent.

For example, in commenting on the prevalence of social pathology in a particular neighborhood, a sociologist might resort to the concept of "anomie." In a most effective way, he might remark, "The high rate of senseless violence stems from what sociologists would call 'anomie,' meaning that the rules of everyday behavior have broken down, causing people to feel confused about what is and is not expected." Thus by this response, one could not only explain a pressing social problem, but also give a mini-lesson in applied sociology.

The Risk of Being Exploited

No matter how well prepared, you may still encounter a few producers or reporters who will not hesitate to exploit you—to use your expertise, pick your brain, edit or misquote you for their own purposes, or perhaps not give you an ounce of credit. We are not suggesting that the industry attracts calloused, unfeeling people. Indeed, most are well-intentioned and talented professionals. The problem is more structural: The norms of behavior in the mass media (the pressures of deadlines, the restrictions on space, the fierce competition, and the need to simplify complex ideas) encourage practices that may not be to your advantage. For example, a reporter, trying to be more provocative than his competitors, may attempt to coerce you into taking a more absolute or extreme position than is comfortable, implying that your statement may not be used otherwise. Or, a producer who is concerned about limited air time may decide not to give your university affiliation in a scripted introduction.

It is important to be aware of the potential risks of exploitation. Getting involved with your eyes open may prevent you from getting blindsided. That is one of the reasons why we wrote this guidebook. Unfortunately, there will be times when there is little, if anything, that you can do to stop it. The only absolute way to prevent yourself from being victimized is to refuse to play the game. But remember, it's the only game in town.

In this chapter we have tried to prepare you for dealing effectively with the media. Now, stay tuned for the news.

**Q&A With
Mary Breslauer**
*Director of
Communications,
Northeastern
University*

Q. What do you see as the primary objective of public relations at the university level?

A. I don't think that the goals of public relations for a university differ much from the goals of public relations in a corporation—to enhance and improve the image and overall reputation of the institution. Within that context, each university, each politician, each corporation has a different set of goals and priorities that it seeks to stress. Obviously, that's your launching pad.

Photo by J. D. Levine, Northeastern University

Q. How does the academic who wants publicity for his or her own work fit into the public relations scheme?

A. It's an important piece of the equation. I think that when you talk about image building it happens successively, and the university or college clearly benefits from having faculty experts. If you are fortunate enough to have a number of faculty members quoted on a number of newsworthy and thought-provoking issues, it begins to build an image of an exciting place to learn and to grow.

Q. What do you think the faculty members get out of it?

A. I believe the faculty members get a lot out of it. They get recognition for their work, being among the public beyond the university walls. If they are lucky enough to work for an enlightened administration, they certainly should receive recognition from the administration. It may not always be equated to dollars, but my experience has been that these are faculty members who, by and large, are treated with an extra measure of respect. Obviously, its a win-win situation to have faculty members who really care greatly about the institution and, therefore, when they have an opportunity also see it as an opportunity for the university. That's when you have a great match.

Q. As a public relations specialist, what do you see as the most important thing that you can do for faculty?

A. If you can be a conduit, that's terrific. First of all, when someone becomes well known, that literally is the principal role that we serve. I also think it's important for us to educate faculty members about what is involved in becoming an expert. And then there is tremendous responsibility on their end as well. That means meeting deadlines and returning phone calls. My greatest frustration is that some faculty members want very much to be stars and indeed are doing more to get the media attention, but they aren't willing to do more to build and maintain connections. They are not willing to be available when you want them. They are not willing to return phone calls with regularity and they want it both ways. And you know what? Those people don't go anywhere. One of the biggest complaints from reporters is that some faculty members don't return phone calls and that they are not being straight with us about their availability. So, I have learned to talk very straightforwardly. I tell them they've got to take all of the calls; and for a lot of them, media training is essential.

Q. Do you provide media training?

A. I am trying now to put a package together that would give media training to a lot of people. You know it's a tough one. Some people get it immediately; some people never get it. You can't make a different personality out of people, but the reality of it is that any academic who is going to be a media star will be talking about things that interest you.

Q. Is there anything that you would like to add?

A. Yes. Academics need to work more closely with the public relations office if they expect to maximize their potential.

3 | The News

Of all forms of media involvement, arguably the most prestigious is the news. Unlike talk shows such as *Geraldo* and *The Oprah Winfrey Show* or feature programs such as *A Current Affair* and *Hard Copy*, which combine entertainment with information and thus are sometimes regarded disparagingly as "Tabloid TV," the news is perceived as highly credible. Thus the opportunity to provide news commentary or to respond to news events will likely give you enhanced status not only in the community but even among your colleagues.

It is ironic, therefore, that the amount and complexity of information you are allowed to contribute tend to vary inversely with the status of the program format. Unlike "soft" entertainment programs in which you often have the chance to elaborate on a point or make several comments, the news operates more on the basis of "sound bites"—brief and colorful phrases that must hold the attention of the viewer. Unfortunately, sound bites tend to be superficial and do not permit the speaker to qualify his or her remarks. For academics who are used to giving verbal footnotes when they speak to classes or colleagues—who are used to saying "yes, under certain conditions" or "not always, but sometimes"—this may take some practice. News producers are looking for clear-cut, definitive answers, not equivocation. Should you attempt to give an overly qualified response in a taped interview, it will likely end up on the editing room floor.

The need for succinct and provocative answers is particularly true of television news, because of the visual dependency of the medium. That is, television news relies heavily on interesting, on-location footage of crimes, fires, and other events with lots of action. In contrast, the time devoted to "talking heads" is restricted, typically to no more than 10 to 15 seconds, because many viewers (perhaps except for PBS audiences) find them a literal "turn-off."

Radio news, on the other hand, is "all talk, no action." Unable to show interesting visuals, radio news programs devote much more time to expert commentary. In addition to the opportunity to exact more air time, radio can afford you several other advantages. Obviously, you don't have to worry about how you look—whether your tie is straight or your hair is in place. Less obvious is the fact that because the audience cannot see what you're doing, you can refer to prepared notes, an outline of major points, or even some catchy phrases scrawled on a napkin.

Least obvious is the convenience factor. With television news, you either must travel down to the station and sit around waiting to go into the studio, or at least have your office (and even your books) rearranged to accommodate the lights and cameras. With radio, all you need is a telephone. A television interview can require more than a half-hour, including set up and take down, just to get 8 seconds of air time. A phone interview for radio lasts a few minutes and may be aired virtually in its entirety.

For many people, particularly those in remote parts of the country, the ubiquity of the telephone allows you to be involved in the national scene. The NBC radio network or the Mutual Radio Network can reach you whether you're in New York City or Walla Walla, Washington. For a television interview to take place, you and the camera must get together, either at their place or yours. Moreover, should a news story break in a locale far away from you—for example, in Juneau,

Alaska—you may get a call from a local radio station there. It is unlikely, however, that you would be contacted by a Juneau television station because of the practical limitations of travel and high cost of satellite transmission.

Live Interviews

Live news interviews force you to be quick on your feet. It is easy, therefore, to put your foot in your mouth if you are not prepared. We find, however, that the spontaneity of a live interview is stimulating in a positive way. Being on the spot forces you to rise to the challenge and may even bring out the best in you.

To make the most of a live interview opportunity and to increase the likelihood that you'll be asked to return, we offer the following general guidelines:

- *Take the "I" out of "I don't know."* Leave that for the classroom. Producers expect you to know—that's why you were called. Of course, you are not expected to be an expert on everything; so if you are totally uncomfortable with the topic, the time to decline is when you are first called for an interview—not when the camera is rolling. During the interview, be prepared to say something meaningful. Where research is lacking, you can say so as long as you also are willing to state an opinion. Rather than looking ignorant, try responding, "Well, the evidence is mixed, but I believe that . . ." or, "We're not sure of x, but we do know y."

- *Come prepared with a set of themes that can be modified as needed.* Feel free to respond to a different question than exactly the one posed. Just because you're asked "a stupid question" doesn't mean you have to give "a stupid answer." Take the opportunity to say something important, even if it doesn't quite fit the question.

- *Don't be afraid to go out on a limb.* Most people are not going to remember precisely what you said as long as you sound like you know what you are talking about. Of course, we are not suggesting that you be deceptive or dishonest in your remarks. But, if you have a position and it is based on sound reasoning or research, then state it forcefully. Don't sound "wishy-washy" simply out of fear of criticism. To be certain that your comments aren't aired, just say, "Well, perhaps it might be so, but I'm not sure that it applies in most cases."

- *In live situations, how you look is not as important as what you say and how you say it, even on television.* Typically, the camera will shoot you with a close up that shows only your face and not always in the best light. Of course, you can smile and nod your head when you're introduced, but there is little else you can do to enhance your appearance.

Taped Interviews

Taped interviews, which are much more common, are far easier to fine-tune. There is much more polish expected in taped interviews, so take advantage of whatever opportunity you have to enhance your presentation of self:

- *Think first.* Before answering a question, feel free to pause and think about your answer or look at your notes. The editor can make it look spontaneous by excising the dead air.

- *Take two.* If you stumble over your words, lose your train of thought, or don't like where your answer is headed, you can always ask the interviewer to let you start over.

- *Interviewers usually welcome suggestions for questions, so come prepared with your best material.* In fact, you will probably be asked at the end of the interview (unless they run out of tape) if you have anything to add. Be their guest.

- *Appearance is vital in taped interviews.* You may be allowed to suggest a camera angle to show off your good side. Sometimes, however, the *interviewer's* good side or the aesthetics of the background setting will take precedence.

- *Stay focused.* Concentrate on what you are saying, regardless of what happens around you. The camera is on you and the tape is rolling. Keep speaking, even if the phone rings, the interviewer rudely pulls out a comb and fixes his hair, or the producer drops his notepad on the floor. You have no control over whether this portion of the interview is ultimately aired or edited out, so assume that it will be used.

News Interview Shows

News interview (or panel) shows, such as *Face the Nation* or *Nightline*, represent the best of two worlds. They offer the high prestige of the news along with the time allotment common to television talk shows. In fact, it is as close as one can get in the electronic media to a genuine, intellectual exchange of ideas. As a result, the usual advice about giving brief and colorful sound bites may not apply; however, it is still important to be direct and forceful in your commentary.

In recent years, particularly with news interview shows, it has become fashionable to question guests "by remote," even when the "far-away" setting is the very next room. ABC's *Nightline*, for example, routinely uses split screen techniques to distance the guests from the interviewer. Being interviewed by remote puts you at a decided disadvantage.

Typically, you are placed in a studio and handed an earpiece to hear the on-air conversation. Without a television monitor (and sometimes without a cameraperson), it is often difficult to determine when a question is directed to you. In a sense, you are blind, that is, you have no visual cues to know when it is appropriate to speak or how others on the show are reacting. You have little control over the flow of the interview.

Because the only connection you have with the conversation is auditory, make sure that the earpiece is firmly lodged in your ear. Under hot lights, it has the tendency to slip out. Also, double-check the volume control and quality of the connection. If you can't hear well, it will tend to show in your answers.

In some debate formats, both opponents are interviewed by remote cameras and thus are equally disadvantaged. On other occasions, however, only one of the guests is interviewed by remote, while others are in the station with the interviewer.

Case Study

A remote hookup turned out to be a significant handicap for one of the authors (Jack) in a debate-style interview on CNN's *Newsmaker Sunday*. Because CNN does not have a Boston bureau, Jack was forced to travel. Out of concern that the return flight to Boston might not be in time for his class, he chose to do a remote interview from CNN's New York bureau rather than to make the longer trip to Washington, D.C., where the show originated.

The other guests were from the Capitol area, and thus appeared in the studio, seated next to the interviewer. The program featured a heated discussion of the role of biology versus environment in the proclivity toward violence. Isolated in the New York studio, Jack felt like an outsider looking in. Lacking a monitor (because of the cost, few programs provide one), he couldn't see the body language and expressions of the other participants and was unable to interrupt when needed without appearing rude. Not until later, when reviewing a tape of the program, did Jack realize just what the audience had seen. To every one of Jack's points, one of the guests who held an opposing perspective reacted with a highly visible smirk. Jack might have responded differently had he been aware of the nonverbal messages (on second thought, he was probably better off not knowing at the time).

<hr>

If you have any choice in the matter, therefore, you are usually far better off making the journey to the station rather than being interviewed by remote. Not only will the interview generally run smoother, but you may be given more airtime as well. Of course, you sometimes have no choice in the matter. Your schedule may not permit making the trip or the producer may not want to spend the money to fly you in for the show. With a fast-breaking news story, moreover, there may not be enough time to do anything but a remote feed.

The Late News

For the academic who wants to use the media to have an impact on society, the news is as frustrating as it is powerful. Even though thousands may be watching, they won't be watching *you* for very long. Is a 10-second picture really worth a thousand words? Not if your purpose is to explain or analyze a situation in any detail. Not if you need to qualify your remarks in any way. Ironically, the most criticized form of electronic media exposure, which is discussed in the next chapter, actually provides the greatest opportunity for academics to elaborate their views. Can we talk?

Q&A With
Ernie Anastos
News Anchor,
WCBS-TV, New York

Q. What do you see as your primary objective as an anchor?

A. My primary responsibility is to inform and to report on a day-to-day basis. So, my main objective is to make sure that I communicate clearly the information and the stories that we are reporting. I also feel that I have to generate some interest. I'd like people to be able to say, "Hey, that's interesting. I didn't know that." I try to give the audience reason to want to learn more about a story—either to read more about it or to watch another program that would give them more depth. I also feel that this might motivate people into action. Sometimes, for example, there are stories that we put on the air that are health related. It could be a political story. Or, it could be a story about social change. The story might motivate members of the audience to say, "I want to get involved. I want to write my congressman. I want to do something about that."

I also think that my role on the air is to give the sense that this is a team effort. I am an anchor but I am also a host. I introduce reporters on the air. I introduce their stories. I also introduce sports and weather. And I introduce specialty reporters, whether they happen to be in the area of money or health or any other particular area.

I also have to set a tone on the air so that there is some stability, so that there is a sense of authority. I have to make mistakes look good. If there is an error—a technical problem or a problem in the copy—I have to be able to finesse things so that someone looking at the broadcast would think, "Gee, that was very smooth. I felt comfortable watching that person."

Q. Would you run through the process of how you produce the news?

A. First of all, it's quite an effort putting a newscast together, and many people are involved. The news director certainly has a say in the direction that the overall news department will take. Assignment managers and producers are part of a group that makes the decision as to what we are going to put on the air. Anchors usually have some input, depending on the kind of "shop" it is. Sometimes, there are producer-oriented shops; sometimes, there are talent-oriented shops. Obviously, if you have a talent shop, you have more say as to what is going on. But I think that most television stations strike a balance. Regarding which stories get put on, I would say there is some agreement between the news director, the executive producer, and the line producer who is responsible for putting it together. They receive input from the assignment manager, who has a sense of which stories will generate interest; which ones will have good visuals, for example. After that, anchors do have, like a lot of other people in the shop, the opportunity to go in and say, "I like this story. Are we including it in this newscast?" In a sense, there is a team effort.

I prepare by making sure that I read enough material to have background on the stories I might be involved with on the air. If there is a live interview coming up, or if there is a breaking story, I need to have a sense of what is going on so that I can ask intelligent questions. In my office, I'll be monitoring CNN most of the time and a local cable operation. I'll flip back and forth, and I kind of keep up with what's going on.

Prior to going on the air, there is a review of the "rundown," which is a list of all the stories that are going on the air. The anchor will sit down with the producers and take a look at the rundown for that particular broadcast. "This is our lead story, this is our feature story, and this is our story before weather." You usually have a sense of what they are about. But you talk to the producer more specifically about something that might be coming up.

Q. How do you see the role of the academic in this process?

A. When we look for experts in a live or taped interview, we look for someone who will provide us with the information we need, who looks good (appearance is important), and who is animated or has some style that is appealing to the viewer. We have our favorites. We go through the Rolodex and we look up someone who might be an expert on a particular subject. We know we like this individual because he or she meets our criteria. They are well informed, and they are going to give you a good sound bite. In a live interview, they don't choke up. They are very relaxed in front of a camera. And they have an appearance that makes them attractive to watch and to listen to. You can also overexpose somebody. So we are careful to rotate our experts. You also need easy access to that individual. It can't be difficult to book somebody. If you call someone and they are not readily available, then they are not used often. You want someone who says, "Oh sure, I can make it. I'll be there in a half-hour."

Q. What advice do you have for academics who want to be involved with the news?

A. Try to get your name into the Rolodex, even if it means sending a letter to someone at the assignment desk or to the news director and being very direct by saying, "I am a professor of so-and-so and am interested in being a part of anything that has to do with this particular subject. If you need me, I think you'd be pleased with what I can offer you."

You can even attend a conference of the radio/television news directors' association. They are held every year and are attended by radio and television news directors from all over the United States. There is another organization, the National Association of Broadcasters, that has meetings where you might meet news directors, presidents, and general managers of stations. The other way for people in the teaching profession to get on the news is to write books and articles, and especially newspaper and magazine articles. The newspaper is the "bible." News staffs go through the newspaper cutting out articles and underlining all the people who are mentioned. If you are in a newspaper or a magazine article, you are almost assured that someone is going to call you.

4 | Talk Shows and Feature Programs

During the past decade, game shows and daytime soap operas have lost much of their popularity to talk and feature shows on both radio and television. One might say that *The Edge of Night* was eclipsed by *Good Morning America*, and *I've Got a Secret* became *Now It Can Be Told*. The changing face of the electronic media has created an unprecedented opportunity for academics to get publicity for their research and books.

Unlike game shows or the soaps, talk shows such as *The Oprah Winfrey Show* and feature programs such as *A Current Affair* regularly focus on topics about which academics from a variety of disciplines can make a contribution. Typically, the format of most of these programs combines personal stories from everyday people with expert analysis from academics and authors. A standard formula involves a panel of victims along with a specialist or two, whether the topic is family violence, drugs, infidelity, disease, or gossip.

Talking Heads

During early years of talk radio, pioneering talkmasters such as Long John Neville, Barry Gray, and Jerry Williams enjoyed small but very devoted audiences. At the same time, Phil

Table 4.1 Nationally Televised Talk Shows

Show	Network/Syndicate	Telephone
A Current Affair	FOX	(212) 452-3500
CBS This Morning	CBS	(212) 975-2824
CBS Sunday Morning	CBS	(212) 975-4114
Dateline NBC	NBC	(212) 664-3888
Donahue	Multimedia	(212) 664-6501
Face the Nation	CBS	(202) 457-4481
48 Hours	CBS	(212) 975-4848
Geraldo	Tribune	(212) 332-0500
Good Morning America	ABC	(212) 456-5900
Hard Copy	Paramount	(213) 373-7200
Inside Edition	King	(212) 737-3399
Jenny Jones	Warner Bros.	(312) 836-9400
Larry King Live	CNN	(202) 898-7900
Nightline	ABC	(202) 887-7360
Nightalk	ABC	(212) 957-5000
Maury Povich	NBC	(212) 989-8800
Primetime Live	ABC	(212) 456-3600
Sally Jessy Raphael	Multimedia	(212) 582-1722
The Joan Rivers Show	Tribune	(212) 975-5522
60 Minutes	CBS	(212) 975-2006
Today	NBC	(212) 664-4249
20/20	ABC	(212) 456-2020
Up to the Minute	CBS	(212) 975-2525
Montel Williams	FOX	(212) 921-9600
The Oprah Winfrey Show	Harpo	(312) 633-0808

Donahue, nationally syndicated from Chicago, had a virtual monopoly of television talk. But then the baby-boom generation—76 million strong—approached middle age, many of them switching from rock to talk. As a result, the talk show market, both on radio and television, grew enormously during the 1980s.

In recent years, a number of popular talk show hosts, such as Larry King, Rush Limbaugh, and Bruce Williams on radio and Geraldo Rivera, Sally Jessy Raphael, and Montel Williams on television, have become syndicated nationally (see listing of national TV talk shows given in Table 4.1). As a consequence, the competition for listeners/viewers and for guests, which is more important from our point of view, has become fierce. They are all looking for experts, including those from academia.

Radio and television talk shows are very different from each other in the kind of role a guest expert can expect to play. On radio, the interview format generally consists of a one-on-one conversation between the host and guest (in person or by phone), supplemented by calls from listeners. As a result, the guest is truly the focal point of the program. This means more time on the air, but also more pressure to answer every question that is posed, no matter how difficult or bizarre.

A few television talk shows, such as CNN's *Larry King Live*, are essentially radio-style talk shows with a camera added. From the guest's point of view, the change in medium does not alter the role (except you have to keep your tie straight). In contrast, most contemporary TV talk shows do not feature an expert guest in a central role.

Nationally syndicated shows such as *The Oprah Winfrey Show* and *Maury Povich* and localized programs such as *People Are Talking* adopt a format to make the most of the medium. Rather than one or two guests, they use a panel that can change from commercial break to commercial break. Rather than invite phone questions from listeners, they take questions from an in-studio audience. As a result, your role is diminished.

On television, your time on the air may be dictated by a producer whose primary concern is with the ratings. You must accept the fact that ordinary people suffering from extraordinary problems get much more time than experts who devote their careers to analyzing those problems. It is conceivable that you may fly across the country to appear on a one-hour, syndicated talk show only to find that you are brought on for the final 8-minute segment of the show. Or you may be assigned to a seat in the first row of the audience and asked to respond once or twice to points made by guests featured on the stage.

This is not to minimize the importance of the expert's role. He or she provides a context for what otherwise might degenerate into pure tabloidism. In addition, academic involvement lends credibility to these programs. Even a few minutes on a national or major-market program is valuable exposure, considering that millions of people will be watching. Plus, do not forget about the reruns. When a program decides to repeat a show on which you appeared, you will reap "residuals" of a sort—extra publicity without extra effort.

We have met a number of experts who complain bitterly about the limited time they receive on television shows. Some people with advanced degrees find it offensive to be overshadowed by a guest whose only claim to fame is having started a club for overweight cross-dressers who cannot find clothes in their size or gender. One particularly irate expert we know recently insisted that he would never again appear on the *The Oprah Winfrey Show* because he was only brought on stage for the final segment. He just didn't think it was worth it.

On television you never get enough time to say everything you wanted or expected to say. First of all, you must accept the reality that the viewing audience finds the trials and tribulations of an incest victim considerably more interesting than the theories expounded by an expert on dysfunctional families. Second, television talk show producers often overproduce a program by inviting more guests than actually are needed. As a result, no one guest has a chance to dominate the discussion. Finally, it is the nature of entertainment television to place drastic limitations on the length of discussions—the last thing a producer wants is for a talk show to seem like Public Broadcasting's *Classroom of the Air.*

You may not be able to control the length of your airtime on television or radio, but you do have some say over the strength. There are actually two sets of concerns that will make you stronger—one deals with how you look, and the other with what you say. Academics, whose commitment is to the development and communication of ideas, are often put off by television's emphasis on image. Unfortunately, perhaps, if you don't look good, the audience won't listen to you; in a visual medium such as television, your credibility is determined as much by your appearance and demeanor as by your academic degrees, professional affiliation, or substantive knowledge. Because television talk shows place a heavy emphasis on entertainment, issues of appearance discussed in the chapter on doing the news become even more critical. In addition, unlike the news for which only a close-up of your face may be briefly shown, TV talk shows portray you in a number of different poses and for an extended period of time.

In terms of both appearance and performance, therefore, the following suggestions are designed to make the most of your airtime:

- *Some academics are surprised and even uncomfortable when an associate producer offers them makeup.* Most national and many local television talk shows have a makeup expert on staff who routinely applies makeup (at least pancake or corn silk) to all guests, unless it is declined. If you are tempted to say no to makeup, consider that the host and probably all the other guests will be made to look healthier than you under the hot lights. Without makeup, you will certainly shine under the spotlight, but not in the way that you would like.

- *Ever since the film* Broadcast News, *male talk show guests routinely sit on their coattails before the camera rolls.* With the same purpose in mind—of looking your best, you should remember always to cross your legs and keep your hands away from your face. In order to appear involved in the conversation, look at the person who is speaking. Do not look at the camera or at the floor. Finally, it is important to be animated, so do not be afraid to gesture with your hands and to shake your head in response to a question.

- *You may have to "audition," even if you do have a Ph.D. and are recognized by your colleagues as an expert in the field.* The first telephone contact you receive from a "booker," an associate producer, or an intern may turn out to be a tryout. Before he or she commits to having you as a guest, the representative will most likely ask a series of questions designed to determine whether you speak clearly and in a way that would be interesting to a wide audience. Thus it is important to recognize that you are "onstage" even though not on camera. Answer questions in the same fluid, enthusiastic, and succinct manner that you would use on the air.

- *Unless you "bomb" (and we know the feeling when it happens), you may then be scheduled for a preinterview over the phone with an associate producer.* The purpose of the preinterview is to provide material for the host who will be interviewing you on the air. This may be your only chance to shape the direction and scope of the program. Thus before he or she calls back, be prepared with a set of topics and questions (with good answers, of course), as if you were producing the show. (Don't expect that the host will necessarily stay with the "script" that you develop in the preinterview.) Another important way to have input into the design of the show is to suggest "case studies"—real people encountered in the process of doing research who might also come on the show and complement what you have to contribute. For example, if you do research on a particular disease, you might be able to recommend someone who has suffered from the illness and will provide a personal story. Despite what we said about competition for time from "real-life" guests, you may at least be able to ensure that these guests are people with whom you are familiar and have good rapport.

- *Make a point during the preinterview to indicate how you wish to be identified on the air.* Some people think to suggest how they would like to be introduced, for example, as a professor from "ABC University" or as the author of a book titled *XYZ: A New Perspective.* Very few know to say how they want to be identified by the "chyron" (the chyron refers to a one- or two-line identifier that appears under your face). Whereas you may be introduced only once, the chyron will appear a number of times throughout the show. Unfortunately, producers do not always recognize the importance of an academic affiliation and are sometimes unwilling to identify an expert with his or her institution. They are much more likely to write "Biologist" under your name, because it's short and more meaningful to the audience than "ABC University." It is not unheard of for your name to be omitted as well. Thus be as forceful as you can in suggesting your preference.

- *If you have a book related to the topic for which you want publicity, make sure that your publisher sends a copy in advance of your appearance.* In fact, some shows request multiple copies of a published book. Even if the book is sent, be sure to bring your own copy with you to the show. Also, remind the producer about identifying or showing the book on the air. Even if your concern is not book sales (perhaps the book has a limited audience or is out of print), being identified with a book will significantly enhance your credibility to the audience.

- *Be prepared to hurry up and wait.* In the academic world, you might get away with being "fashionably late" for class or a faculty meeting—"better late than never." But on the talk show circuit, late is always too late. In fact, most producers will insist that you arrive at least an hour before the show. Certainly you need some time for makeup, microphone checks, and meeting the other guests, but for the most part, producers expect you to arrive very early so that they don't have to worry about a "no show."

- *Have a stale doughnut and some cold coffee.* The "green room" is where guests are told to wait, relax, and have a snack prior to going out on the set. There are several different explanations for how the green room (which usually is not painted green) derived its name. Most suggest something about the complexion of a guest's face either from stage fright or from having eaten too many of the scrumptious jelly doughnuts. (Some guests are too nervous to eat, while others eat because they are nervous.) While in the green room, you will likely be asked to sign a "release," which absolves the show and the station from any legal responsibility for your errors. Most guests sign without reading it. Even though the language is pretty standard, we suggest that you at least skim the release for objectionable items. In rare cases, guests have been allowed to pencil in specific changes before signing.

- *Keep the preshow chatter light.* The green room also provides an opportunity to make small talk with other guests on the show. In general, you should try to avoid discussing the substance of the remarks that you intend to make on the air. For one thing, you may come to feel during the actual interview like you are repeating yourself and therefore be unnecessarily reticent on air. Also, in an adversarial exchange, you might disadvantage yourself by providing your opponent with a preview of your arguments.

- *When the show begins, it is important to appear spontaneous, even if your responses to questions have been prepared in advance.* And even if your style of dress is formal, a certain degree of informality of speech is desirable. Thus it is useful to begin (and only begin) an answer with verbal fillers, such as "Well" or "You know."

- *Bad questions deserve good answers.* In talk shows that have live audiences or call-ins, you will often be posed a question that is virtually impossible to answer directly. It may be a question that was already answered. It may be an ill-conceived question (for example, a caller asking without a context, "What about Charles Manson?"). Or it may be a question that is unclear or unintelligible. Regardless of the question, you have the mike. Use it to say something you really want to get into the conversation, even if it doesn't quite fit.

- *Be aggressive without being obnoxious.* Producers prefer having a lively exchange rather than a series of "speeches" from guests. In fact, just before the show, the host or producer may encourage all of the guests not to wait to be called upon, but to speak right up and even to interrupt if necessary.

- *It's live or it might as well be.* Unlike taped face-to-face interviews that are edited, talk shows almost never give you a second chance at answering a question. Some shows, radio and TV, are live, although they may operate on a delay to prevent obscenities from going out on the air. Taped shows have the capacity for "retakes," but almost never do so, unless, of course, the *host* stumbles through his opening lines.

Features

The television feature program or news magazine is another form of talk show that has grown in popularity. Always on tape, feature programs contain a series of topic segments and involve a structured format, combining news footage with interviews. Thus they can be characterized as a cross between news and talk.

Because they contain elements of both news and talk programs, the advice we can give for participating in feature programs combines suggestions relating to both kinds of shows. As with taped news interviews, you should try to be succinct in your remarks and provocative in your message. As with talk shows, on the other hand, you have the time in advance to prepare both your appearance and your commentary.

Unlike newscasts, which are fairly standard in their format, feature programs vary considerably in their approach, from hard-hitting exposé to light on-air gossip. If at all possible, prepare for an interview by watching an episode of the program beforehand.

Case Study

The importance of becoming familiar with theme and format applies both to talk shows for which you should preview the style of the interviewer as well as to feature programs for which you should be aware of the show's perspective. Both of us learned this lesson the hard way from appearances on CBS's *48 Hours,* a weekly documentary-style program in which reporters cover several stories all on a particular theme "as they happen."

For an episode titled "Serial Killing," Jamie was featured in a segment focusing on his role in the investigation of an unsolved serial murder spree in Gainesville, Florida. He was followed by camera from his office in Boston, to crime scenes in Gainesville, to the home of a grieving family in Miami. Over a 4-day period, he was repeatedly asked a number of challenging and probing questions, often in a skeptical tone. Not familiar with the perspective of the program, Jamie became somewhat guarded in his responses, suspecting that the interviewer was trying to make him look bad. Had he watched the program beforehand, he would have known that he had the "wrong number"—this was *48 Hours,* not *60 Minutes;* cinema verite, not investigative journalism. Although he was very pleased with the result when it aired, he could have enjoyed the experience more than he did.

A few months later, for an episode called "Massacre," Jack appeared in a segment of *48 Hours* about the 1991 mass murder of 23 people in Killeen, Texas. For two days, the camera followed him around the Northeastern University campus, into his office and classrooms, and finally to his car at the end of the day. Instructed by the producer not to stage anything, that the show was "cinema verite," Jack conducted "business as usual." Had he been more familiar with the show, he would have guessed that the producer *really* wanted interesting interactions related to the topic of the program, so long as they didn't look staged or contrived. As it turned out, the aired segment was fine, but was limited to scenes of Jack lecturing to his students and being interviewed by a *48 Hours* correspondent.

Publicizing Your Book

The overwhelming majority of books produced by academics—textbooks and scholarly monographs—are simply not appropriate for the talk show circuit. Of course, there are many research publications that contain provocative ideas or newsworthy information. Thus you may find that the results reported in your recent monograph provide fertile ground for a series of newspaper or public affairs interviews. But even the most important book may not have the mass appeal necessary to be distributed widely in national bookstore chains or become a best-seller. As a practical matter, there is little point in having Phil Donahue or Geraldo Rivera hold your book to the camera, when only your colleagues and students (and parents) are likely to buy it.

By contrast, some academics have written books that cross the line dividing scholarly publishing from its trade and mass-market counterparts. Television and radio talk shows rely heavily on these books and their authors to provide program ideas and guests. With the objective in mind of appealing to a mass audience, or at least an audience of educated laypersons, there are some helpful suggestions for "pushing" your book outside of the academic world.

- *If people don't know about it, they won't buy it.* No matter how much appeal your book has, it will likely still need an effective media campaign to succeed in the marketplace. The campaign might involve a regional or national book tour of radio and television talk shows. If you're lucky, your publisher, or perhaps even your university, will agree to underwrite in full or in part the travel costs of your tour. At minimum, your publisher should be willing to supply media outlets with review copies of your book. You can still stage an effective and inexpensive "tour by telephone" of radio talk shows around the country with perhaps one or two television shows included.

- *Don't forget to call Sally, Maury, and Phil.* Fortunately for authors, the tremendous growth in the number and popularity of national television and radio talk shows has reduced the necessity for extended travel from city to city to deliver the message. The national talk shows have plenty of money to pay for your travel expenses, even if you're trying to publicize your book. A positive endorsement of your book on the *The Oprah Winfrey Show* or *Larry King Live* is worth weeks of tedious and expensive travel for appearances on local programs around the country.

- *If people can't find it, they won't buy it.* All the publicity in the world will not make a difference if potential readers cannot locate your book in their local bookstore. A motivated few might special order it, but hardly enough to justify the investment of time and money needed for a book tour. Of course, publicity can stimulate the distribution of your book. For example, a scheduled appearance on the *The Oprah Winfrey Show* will help your publisher's sales representatives in convincing bookstores to stock your title. Thus keep your publisher informed of all media bookings.

- *Get the word out.* A critical step in assembling an effective campaign is to flood the media with promotional material concerning your book. Talk show producers should receive a flier announcing the publication of your book, a phone contact for receiving a publicity copy, and a schedule of times when you are available for an interview. In addition, producers of programs on your priority list (such as the national shows plus the larger local shows) should, as a matter of course, be sent a copy of the book.

If your book appeals to a specialized audience (for example, single adults), work with your publisher to target the right media people.

- *Choose wisely and carefully.* When requests for interviews start coming in, be aware that many shows insist on "first appearance" within their market. For example, if you are booking radio talk shows in Chicago, you may be told by the producers of several shows that you are free to appear on any other radio program in the city, as long as they are first. The same goes for the nationally syndicated television talk shows. In fact, some national programs make you sign an agreement that you will not appear on any of their competitors for a specified period of time. Thus be realistic. Don't turn down a top show, waiting for *the* top show.

- *Wait for the right time.* Despite the temptation to go public with an idea that you feel is important, it is best not to do any interviews for at least 3 months prior to the publication of your book. Most national and local talk shows have an unwritten rule about not using "overexposed" guests or topics. Even if a producer "promises" to have you on again when your book is out, you cannot be sure that it will happen.

Talk Is Not Cheap

The now defunct *Morton Downey Show* may have adversely colored the image held by millions of Americans regarding television talk. It is true that major syndicated talk shows at least occasionally feature trivial, silly, stupid, or offensive topics and guests. Despite the criticism, however, they often present more in-depth analysis of important political and social issues than primetime TV or even the news. As an academic, therefore, you will appreciate the expanded opportunity to explain your point of view that this format provides.

**Q&A With
Bill Lancaster
*Producer,
The Geraldo Show***

Q. What is your primary objective in producing a nationally syndicated talk program?

A. My objective is similar to that of a television reporter. My job is to produce shows about people and events that are in the news. Virtually any subject is a possibility—gays in the military, AIDS discrimination, inner-city gang violence. We cover the gamut from A to Z. We tend to be more news oriented than most other talk shows because of Geraldo's background in journalism. But reporting on the news is only part of the picture. Talk shows have become an integral part of our culture. They perform a myriad of functions. They can be a forum for presidential candidates, a psychiatrist's couch for the troubled, a podium that gives the disenfranchised a voice, or a larger-than-life soap opera. In a sense, you could say my objective as a talk show producer changes every day.

Q. Would you run through the steps in the process of producing a show?

A. Our ideas are generated the way that any reporter's or writer's ideas are generated—through research. We read magazines and newspapers. We watch other television shows. We talk to as many people as we can. Being in New York City is a resource in itself. We find many of our stories just blocks from our office. Each of the producers pitches his or her ideas to the senior producer and the executive producer. We sit down in a conference room at least three times a week and go around the table. Each producer will pitch two or three ideas. You are "yeaed" or "nayed" on the spot.

What happens most often is that the original show idea is amended. Someone will come in and they'll say, "Let's do a show about AIDS." Geraldo will say, "Everyone in America is doing a show about AIDS. How is ours going to be different?" I might respond, "How about AIDS discrimination—for example, kids with AIDS [who are] ostracized at school?" The next stage is to begin seeking the guests. We work a lot with professionals—such as clinicians, professors, psychologists, and psychiatrists. We'll ask them if they have a client who is willing to go on the show.

Suppose we call an AIDS hospital looking for a female patient. A doctor might say, "Well, I have four female patients, all teenage girls who contracted it through blood transfusions." We will ask the patients if they want to do the show. If they agree, we might want to do a videotape. We might send out a crew to film the girls at work or at play, then add that element to the program.

Ninety-nine percent of what I do—and what every talk show producer in America does—is to find interesting and intriguing people. Every producer here has a small staff to rely on. For example, I have an associate producer and interns, so I certainly do have help. But the buck stops with the producer. I'm usually the one sitting at my desk eating Chinese food out of a carton at 1 a.m.

Q. How do you see the role of the academic? How do you select them, and what do you look for?

A. In the talk show business, academics are referred to as "experts." They are generally asked to help clarify the finer points of the day's topic. Most of the time the experts we seek are psychologists or psychiatrists who try to counsel a guest right on the show. When it works, it is a fascinating process. The psychiatrist can elicit intriguing responses from the guest. They can also ask questions that the talk show host might not feel comfortable asking. The experts are often a vital part of the show.

Again, because we deal with so many topics, we seek experts from a wide variety of disciplines. In past shows, our experts have discussed everything from the ethics of fetal tissue transplants to Kennedy assassination theories.

Q. Do you have any advice for an academic who wants to be on talk shows?

A. The biggest thing is to be reachable—travel with a beeper if you want to do talk shows. Second, be available at a moment's notice. Third, be able to speak with great brevity, conciseness, and clarity. The academic will not have as much time as the other guests. Typically, an expert on a talk show will be asked only three questions. The expert, however, can and does play a pivotal role. A well-timed and well-placed observation by an expert can change the course of a show.

5 | Print Media

Talk shows prefer to feature sensational topics that will be entertaining to mass audiences. TV newscasts focus on crime and politics, not to mention weather and sports. Perhaps like many academics, your life's work fits none of these categories. It may be as esoteric as the study of the social organization of penguins in Antarctica. You doubt that Oprah will be calling, or that the 6 p.m. newscast will want an interview. But the daily newspaper may still be a realistic possibility for gaining publicity.

Daily papers offer something for everyone. In addition to news about world, national, and local events, you can often find sections and specialized reporters devoted to science, business, learning, living, and health. Thus you do not necessarily have to wait for a news event to offer your expert commentary or reaction; you can "make the news" by keeping in touch with the appropriate reporters.

Being quoted in the newspaper may not be as glamorous as an appearance on a syndicated TV talk show. After all, you will not be recognized and approached by strangers on the street who say they saw your name in the newspaper. The newspaper is also not as far reaching as the TV news. Although most people read the paper, they read it selectively and thus will not necessarily see your contribution.

Despite these limitations, the newspaper has some important advantages over the electronic media related to its permanence. Many people keep the newspaper around the house for hours, if not days; thus your audience does not have to be "tuned in" at the right time and the right station to see you. You can keep on file articles in which you are quoted, for whatever purpose you might want them (if only to impress your mother).

More important, while television news may have greater credibility with the general public, the newspaper tends to be more highly regarded among your peers. Thus your colleagues and your dean may be more impressed if you are quoted in the daily newspaper than if you appear on the local newscast.

Also, journalists (and other media people) regularly use earlier newspaper articles in researching new ones. They may search their own newspaper library or a national newspaper database service (such as NEXUS) to find experts in a particular area. Many reporters maintain and update a Rolodex containing a list of experts in various fields by monitoring who has been quoted by other reporters. Thus a single interview with a journalist can potentially snowball into dozens, if not hundreds, of other references to your work or ideas. Occasionally, you may be requoted in a secondary source (perhaps without your even being aware of it). More commonly, you may get calls from other reporters looking for similar but fresh statements to quote.

When the Reporter Calls

Your involvement with a newspaper will most often begin with an unexpected phone call from a reporter inquiring about a topic related to your expertise. A breaking news story, however, should alert you to the possibility (and, once your name gets around, the probability) that you will be called for an interview; so be prepared to give your "instant" analysis.

At times, your university public relations office might receive a call from a journalist working on a particular story for which he or she needs an expert opinion. The PR representative will then call you to see if you can and wish to contribute to the article. If so, phone numbers will be exchanged (and the PR department will gladly take credit for making the connection).

The following considerations apply specifically to dealing with newspaper reporters:

- *Newspaper deadlines are typically measured in minutes and hours, not days.* A phone message returned "tomorrow" is usually not worth returning. Morning newspapers, particularly large ones, have early evening deadlines. Thus their reporters usually work on a late morning to early evening schedule. It may be past office hours for you, but you should still try to return a call into the evening. Even if the reporter has finished his or her story by quoting another expert source, there still may be time to slip in a short comment from you.

- *As with all media, accessibility is a key factor in getting publicized.* Given the irregular schedules of both reporters and academics, it may be crucial to be reachable at home. Consider informing the PR office and your own department about guidelines for home contact by media.

- *Get as many facts as possible before you respond to a reporter's questions.* Particularly with breaking news stories, the reporter will generally know more of the "whats" than you do. Before giving the "whys," be wise enough to ask as many questions as possible. You want to avoid making a speculation contradicted by available facts of which you are unaware.

- *Just keep talking.* Unlike television and radio interviews in which you have to be concerned with being succinct and articulate, interviews with newspaper reporters are really conversations. You can repeat yourself, rephrase things, go off on tangents, interrupt, and even reconsider and retract opinions. The reporter will sift through a lengthy interview to find a few choice phrases to quote. Most reporters will also clean up your grammar (whether you like it or not).

- *At the same time, don't be completely unguarded.* Assume that everything is "on the record." Even if you say that something is "off the record," you run the risk of seeing it in print. In fact, the reporter might try to convince you that whatever you just leaked won't hurt and is critical to the story. For the most part, reporters from reputable newspapers can be trusted about taking something off the record. However, if you want to be sure, just don't say it.

- *Don't be surprised when you see your remarks in print.* Even after a lengthy interview, only a small portion of your comments (perhaps one or two quotes) will likely be used. Those statements that do make the story may not be the ones that you would have selected as the highlights of the interview. Don't be upset that your "best stuff" was ignored; just feel fortunate if you are quoted accurately and you are included in the story at all. There is always the chance that nothing you said will be used, that your opinion will be used but not attributed to you, or that the story will be canceled altogether.

News Services

For someone seeking publicity for their work, being called by a reporter from a wire service or news service is cause for excitement. Depending on the particular service involved, a single, 5-minute interview with a reporter from a service as pervasive as the Associated Press (AP) or Reuters can potentially be published in dozens, if not hundreds, of newspapers nationwide and around the world.

Just because you get on the national wire, however, doesn't necessarily mean that the story will be "picked up" by the nation's most prominent newspapers. To the contrary, smaller newspapers, having limited budgets and staff to track down stories, rely more heavily on items "on the wires" to fill pages. Large papers prefer to send their own reporters, even to distant places, in order to get an exclusive story or angle.

Smaller papers, which do not operate with full staffs on the weekends, depend even more on wire stories for their expanded Sunday editions. In fact, the AP provides a large block of feature stories (e.g., "soft" news, follow-ups on events of the week, and profiles) specifically for this purpose. Academic research that has widespread appeal or application is especially likely to be highlighted on the weekend wires.

Of course, not all news services are as ubiquitous as the AP. There are numerous smaller national services (e.g., Scripps-Howard News Service); regional services (including regional AP wire services); international services; as well as topic-specialized services for business, religion, sports, and other matters. Finally, several major newspapers (e.g., *The New York Times*, the *Los Angeles Times*, and the *Washington Post*) operate their own syndicated news services that they sell to smaller papers in their network.

Case Study

In 1983, just when we were beginning to report the findings of our research on mass murderers, we made contact with AP reporter Fred Bayles, who had a keen interest in multiple homicide. We talked with him about the profile of the mass killer from our analysis of 42 case studies. Bayles was as surprised as we were to learn that the typical mass murderer was "extraordinarily ordinary" in appearance—specifically, a white, middle-aged male who was a little bit short, slightly overweight, and with a small mustache (at that time, a small mustache was considered stylish).

At the end of the interview, Bayles remarked, "Now you will see the power of the AP." And, as it happened, he wasn't exaggerating. Our research was publicized in literally hundreds of newspapers across the country, from major metropolitan areas to locations we still can't find on the map. But that was only the beginning. This article repeatedly surfaced during subsequent years whenever reporters researched articles associated with new cases of mass killing.

Press Releases

Suppose that a news event has captured public attention, and you have something new and important to say about it. You don't have to wait by the phone hoping that a reporter doing a story about the topic will call for a quote. You can be proactive, perhaps with the help of your school's public relations office or through the media contacts that you have developed in the past. Don't feel bashful about calling a reporter ("cold" or through a referral) if you can offer some insight about the event. The reporter is likely scanning his or her Rolodex for someone with expertise to comment, and thus your initiative will be appreciated. You might feel worse about missing an opportunity to be in the news than about being told "no, thanks."

It is not even necessary to wait for a news event related to your expertise. Suppose you believe that your new research or perspective on an issue will have widespread interest. You can actually generate the news by contacting a reporter specifically chosen because of the kind of stories he or she writes and by sharing your ideas. Keep in mind, however, that it is not always easy to reach a particular reporter. If on deadline, they will be too busy to talk to anyone. Most will, of course, be willing to return a phone or voice-mail message when the call is from an academic at a local university.

Case Study

How do you find the right reporter for your particular story idea? Several years ago, one of us (Jack) had just completed a series of research projects on gossip and rumor. He thought that the findings were newsworthy, but didn't know a reporter who would necessarily agree to do a story about the research. Calling a reporter with whom he had dealt several times on an entirely different topic (murder), Jack was given the name of a journalist who specialized in soft news. Within 24 hours, the journalist called Jack and later interviewed him in person. The story and an accompanying photograph ran on the AP "Weekend Edition" and appeared in dozens of newspapers across the country.

Contacting a reporter by phone is actually an informal version of a press release. A formal press release is a written, 1- to 2-page summary of your research findings, book, or ideas that is sent widely to print as well as to electronic media. As an advantage over just calling a reporter, a press release has the potential for reaching a significant number of media outlets. In addition, you don't run the risk of being embarrassed by a personal rejection on the telephone.

If brief and well written (in fact, written like a news story), your press release may be published as is or excerpted in part. Or, the release may stimulate sufficient interest so that a reporter will call for an in-depth interview.

Your public relations office may assist you in preparing a press release—indeed, they may even write it for you. But a few simple guidelines can be offered (see sample press release on juvenile homicide that generated several hundred placements):

N Northeastern University

Release

Immediate

Date
October 14, 1992

Phone
617-437-5426
Contact

Terry Yanulavich
Mary Breslauer

NORTHEASTERN UNIVERSITY EXPERTS IDENTIFY STARTLING TRENDS IN VIOLENT CRIME

Juveniles and young adults are committing murder and violent crimes in the U.S. at higher rates than ever before, even as demographic reports show they now make up a smaller percentage of the population, a Northeastern University analysis of FBI crime statistics has revealed.

In addition, only towns with fewer than 10,000 people experienced little or no increase in violent crime between 1985 and 1991 when the homicide rate rose 24 percent and violent crime jumped by 36 percent.

Criminal homicide arrest rates for adult and juvenile males rose by as much as 217 percent for 15-year-olds. The phenomenon is widespread geographically, according to the analysis conducted by Center for Applied Social Research Director Glenn Pierce and Criminal Justice Dean James Fox.

"This rise is alarming because the most violence prone portion of the population, 18-to-24 year-olds, declined during the 80s," said Pierce. "Between 1980 and 1991, the percentage of 18-to-24 year-olds dropped from 13.2 percent of all residents to 10.4 percent.

"We had expected to see a decrease in violent crime as the numbers dropped, but the age dividend never materialized," he added. "It appears that fewer teenagers and young adults are accounting for a greater proportion of crime and the perpetrators are younger. Sixteen-to-20-year-olds are committing murder at a much higher rate."

Pierce and Fox found that during the first half of the 1980's arrests for criminal homicide declined for all age groups to a 15-year low with the trend completely reversing for young adult and juvenile males after 1985. During the decade, the number of prison inmates rose to an historic high of 823,000, a 67 percent increase.

"Clearly we have become a more violent society," said Fox. "The recent wave of youth violence cannot be explained away as a function of demographic shifts or changes in criminal justice policy. Compared with their parents when they were teenagers, the new youth generation has more dangerous drugs in their bodies, more deadly weapons in their hands and are being socialized into a culture having a far more casual attitude toward violence."

-30-

**PLEASE SEE ATTACHED DETAILED ANALYSIS COMPLETE WITH TABLES AND GRAPHS.

Office of University Communications
271 Huntington Avenue, Suite 220
Northeastern University
Boston, Massachusetts 02115

Figure 5.1. Sample Press Release. Used with permission from Northeastern University, Office of University Communications.

- *Use the standard format.* In the top-left corner, indicate the release date (for example, "For Immediate Release" or "Not for Release before Tuesday, January 2, 1999"). Beneath the release date, specify the contact person (you or your PR representative) along with phone numbers. Next, center the title—one that is likely to attract attention. The body of the release should begin with a strong lead paragraph that gives the central finding and implication (the "punchline") derived from your research. The subsequent paragraphs, which provide some details of the research, should be written like a newspaper article (the "who, what, where, why, when, and how") and not a journal article. Finally, attach a one-paragraph biography emphasizing your expertise in the subject matter of the release.

- *Distribute the press release widely within the target area.* Using a directory of media outlets (such as the *Gale Directory of Publications and Broadcast Media*, available in your library), send the release to as many assignment editors, reporters, and producers as possible.

- *If possible, be strategic in your selection of a release date.* You can obviously tie a press release to the date of publication of a book or journal article. You may also conveniently associate a press release with an anticipated event of wide interest, such as the anniversary of a discovery or an annual holiday. Even more to your advantage is to schedule a press release to coincide with a known slow news day. For example, newspaper editors often find it difficult to fill their pages on the days immediately following major holidays, such as Labor Day or Memorial Day. Not only is there no business or political news in the aftermath of the holiday, but most staff reporters had the day off. Therefore, sending a release several days in advance but specifying a release date for the morning after the holiday will present the editor with an ideal opportunity to fill his news void. He or she may even publish the entire press release as is.

Finally, if you do not wish to prepare a special press release, there are more routine mechanisms for alerting the print media to your recent work. As you might do with colleagues, you can send out to selected reporters and editors who regularly deal with your subject matter copies of your papers and reprints of your articles. For example, science writers at major newspapers like to keep current with the scholarly literature and with "who's who" in the field; they might appreciate receiving your latest work and perhaps would want to interview you about it. In recognition of the receptivity of the media to scholarly research, many professional societies set up press rooms at their annual meetings and encourage presenters to be available to members of the media.

Magazines

Many of the suggestions given above for speaking with newspaper reporters also apply to dealing with magazine reporters and writers, both staff and free lance. Specifically, you have little control over how your words are characterized—if you will be quoted correctly and in what context. The fact that magazines are not published daily, but rather weekly or monthly, means that their deadlines are somewhat more flexible. They still operate on a tight schedule, however, so be prompt in returning phone calls. Remember: "Time waits for no man"; neither does *Newsweek*.

Similar to academic journals, magazines can be archived and indexed, giving them permanence and accessibility, unequaled by newspapers. In addition, magazines look better on a coffee table and fit better in a bookshelf than does the daily paper. Plus, magazines don't yellow.

A few special comments regarding magazine interviews are noteworthy:

- *By design, magazines tend to produce more material than they print.* An editor of a news magazine might assign a story focus to several reporters or bureaus that essentially compete for space in the same article. Consequently, even if your remarks are considered important to the reporter who interviews you, the editor might go with the material submitted by a reporter from another bureau. As another form of overproduction, both news and feature magazines will often assign more articles than can be used in an issue, just in case certain stories do not turn out to be as interesting as expected. Thus you may be featured, but in a story that gets "axed."

- *Be aware of the distinction between a staff writer and a free-lancer.* An interview with a staffer (editor or writer) is likely to end up in print. Feature magazines (such as *Redbook* and *Gentlemen's Quarterly*) also publish at least a few stories researched and written by free-lancers. When a free-lance writer calls and says that he or she is doing a story for *Ladies' Home Journal*, several possible situations may prevent publication. First of all, the free-lancer might just be hoping to write for *Ladies' Home Journal*, but not yet have a contract. In addition, although under contract, a project may never be completed, may be completed but not accepted by the editor, or may be accepted by the editor but get "killed" somewhere down the line. How do you tell whether a writer is on staff? Just ask.

- *Check please!* Although it doesn't happen all the time, many magazines employ "fact checkers" who call back to verify quotes, spelling of names, and affiliations. Not only does this minimize the risk of being misquoted, but it also gives you another chance to modify your statements, both in substance and grammar. Virtually all newspapers, even the most prestigious, don't bother to authenticate by checking with the source. Perhaps the best thing of all about being called by a fact checker is that you can be sure that the story is ready for publication; you can even find out in what issue the article is scheduled to run.

Supermarket Tabloids

Many, if not most, academics feel that they are above being quoted in a supermarket tabloid such as the *National Enquirer*, the *Star*, the *National Examiner*, and the *Globe*. The prevailing opinion is that "the tabs" either slant the truth or fabricate it entirely. Yet, in an effort to enhance their credibility, these publications actively seek expert testimony from academics regarding a range of topics, from murder to medicine.

Despite their negative reputation, at least in certain circles, these four tabloids have a combined readership of 10 million people, easily more then *The New York Times* or *USA Today*. Thus the tabloids offer a significant potential for reaching millions in the so-called pink-collar market—middle-aged home-makers with less than a college education. Moreover, most of the gory "two-headed baby" stories have been eliminated by at least the leading tabloids in an effort to attract mainstream advertising.

Thus the potential benefit to these national publications can be attractive. In fact, many academics have had positive experiences dealing with staff reporters from supermarket tabloids. Their comments have been reported accurately and in a favorable context. Similar to more reputable magazines, some tabloids now employ fact checkers who verify quotes from their sources before printing a story.

At the same time, the risks are still great enough to warrant a note of caution. In particular, don't get "strung along." Tabloids often use a number of "stringers"—freelancers who write on a repeated but irregular basis—to fill their pages. Even a tabloid with ethics may have little control over how a stringer deals with you. Recognizing that academics and other experts would refuse to be interviewed for a tabloid, some unscrupulous stringers misrepresent themselves over the phone. For example, we have known tabloid stringers to claim that they work for a foreign publication (speaking with an appropriate British accent, of course) or for an obscure news service that turns out to be the parent company for a "tab." For an academic who spends an hour on the phone and expects to be quoted in the *London Sunday Times,* it can be both disappointing and disturbing to wind up instead sharing a page with the woman who gave birth to a black sheep.

The Back Page

Because of the increasing competition for readers, more and more newspapers have broadened their scope to include a wider variety of articles, not just those on politics or current events. As a result, academics from anthropology to zoology are more likely today to find a place in the news.

Q&A With Chris Lavin
Feature and Science Editor, St. Petersburg Times

Q. What do you see as the reporter's primary objective?

A. There are multiple levels of our objectives. The overriding objective is to bring light to the major issues of the day— the important issues that need to be examined and probed. If you are dealing with authorities, like the police or some elected official, your objective is to scrutinize their performance. Moving down the line, another objective is to tell a good and interesting story and to be entertaining enough to grab the attention of the readers. In this way, they will hopefully consider some of the important subjects that need to be considered.

Q. Would you run through the process of reporting the news?

A. Generally, ideas for stories come from a lot of different areas—sometimes from publicists, from news events and spin-offs from news events, or from natural occurrences such as hurricanes and tornadoes. Once you get an idea, you do research to see what's known about it. In some ways, the reporter's work is not unlike the academic who gets an idea, goes to the existing literature to see what's been done, and looks for a niche—some aspect of the area that hasn't been covered well. You like to deal with things that are new and add to our knowledge, the same way that an academic does. From there, you start making phone calls to experts in the field. You set aside X number of hours to amass as much information as you can. As you move along, you try to hone your idea, focus it much more, eliminating some areas of possible investigation because you see them as less fruitful than others. Then you get to the writing part. You have to write with an eye toward your audience and the subject, attempting somehow to be true to both. That is, you try to make it interesting but keep it factually correct. If you've done everything right, it can be both.

Q. How do you see the role of the academic in this process?

A. The academics are one of the great crutches of American journalism. The rule that drives journalism is "best source." In a lot of areas that are new and at the edge of understanding, academics are farther in front. They have the ability to speak, in some ways like an elected official, with some authority because they are recognized through their doctorate and through their position on the faculty as being a source of some credibility. We look to academics for a deeper understanding than journalists who drop in and out of subjects. The demand for an academic who has chosen an area of study that is interesting to the general public is neverending.

Q. Do you have any advice for academics in dealing with reporters?

A. The problem with some academics is that they don't understand that the journalist needs a clear voice speaking to them. Sometimes academics haven't ferreted out what they can say definitively about a subject. Journalists need a clear voice saying in understandable, relatively simple English, what the state of knowledge is. Too many academics have trouble translating their work to a level that is understandable to the average person on the street. Like a good teacher, the academic should be able to speak to both graduate students and introductory students who lack background in the field.

6 | Op-Ed Columns

The op-ed column, or simply "op-ed" (short for opposite the editorial page), comes closer to traditional scholarship than any other form of media involvement. Thus for many academics, the opportunity to write op-ed columns will be a comfortable avenue for widespread dissemination of scholarly ideas.

Many of the control limitations that might dissuade academics from addressing a public audience through the mass media do not apply to op-ed columns. Unlike being cited or quoted by a newspaper reporter, the words in the op-ed column are of your own choosing (aside from routine copyediting that ordinarily you will not have an opportunity to review or approve). Unlike contributions to radio or television, you can fine-tune your prose into a well-crafted article. Moreover, although some restrictions still apply, you generally have ample space to develop your argument in a cohesive and organized way. Although catchy phrases are still desirable in an op-ed, you do not have to worry about producing just "one-liners" and simple sentences.

In addition to the lack of disadvantages common to other forms of media, there are also some clear-cut advantages to publishing op-ed columns. Most notably, an op-ed is a publication. Thus it definitely belongs on your curriculum vitae, most appropriately listed not among traditional journal articles, but under "Other Publications" or eventually even "Op-Ed Columns."

Another important benefit to submitting op-ed columns is that you will usually get quick feedback—most newspapers make decisions on op-eds in a matter of days, if not hours. Even though the kind of reaction you get from an op-ed editor is essentially nothing more detailed than either "It will appear probably next Tuesday" or "I'm sorry, but we can't use your piece," at least you are not kept hanging for months as with academic journals. In addition, the quick turnaround in publication means more immediate gratification from seeing your ideas in print. Indeed, this can be even more personally rewarding than seeing your journal article in print months or years after the work was central in your thinking. Finally, the modest financial reward (usually in the range of $50 to $150, depending on the size and circulation of the newspaper) will at least pay for a night on the town to celebrate the publication.

Case Study

Op-ed columns have the potential for reaching key decision makers, sometimes pressuring them to implement change. A couple of years ago, we published a column in *The Boston Globe* in which we discussed the growing tension between urban universities and residents in their surrounding communities. To illustrate the point of the piece, we cited specific violent incidents at several universities and recommended that scholarship aid be targeted for promising local youth. Although we may have offended these particular institutions (and were criticized for it), one of the schools—a prestigious Ivy League academy—announced a few weeks later the very type of scholarship program that we advocated. Perhaps this was a coincidence—but perhaps not.

Giving Your Opinion

Op-ed submissions should range in length from 500 to 750 words, although a few newspapers will publish shorter or longer pieces. Most important arguments can surely be made in this amount of space. In addition to the submission, you should send your mailing address, phone number, and social security number (in case of acceptance). Also, you should provide a one-sentence "tag," giving your title, affiliation, and possibly a relevant publication, in order to establish for the reader your credentials. You may choose to attach a brief paragraph or one-page bio for the benefit of the editor. Finally, a few newspapers will ask for a "head shot" photo upon acceptance of your piece, so be sure to have one available.

Not all newspapers accept op-ed columns from free-lance contributors. Most small- and medium-size newspapers publish syndicated columns exclusively. Most larger newspapers (see Table 6.1) do consider unsolicited free-lance submissions, but the competition is fierce. Not only are you vying with possibly hundreds of other free-lance contributors, but most of the space on the page is reserved for regular columnists and editors on staff as well as a host of syndicated columnists.

In order to provide a directory of op-ed editors, we surveyed by mail-questionnaire the opinion-page editors from approximately 100 major newspapers around the country. Table 6.1 (at the end of this chapter) displays the responses of the 70% who completed the survey, including newspaper and editor names, address, phone/fax, how frequently freelancers are used and to what extent local authors are preferred, circulation, geographic exclusivity rights, manuscript length, and payment. We also queried the respondents concerning general submission guidelines and recommendations to freelancers. Based on these and our own experiences in the op-ed market, we can suggest a number of tips to consider that will hopefully increase your chances of success:

- *Call the op-ed editor to discuss an idea.* If you feel uncomfortable making a cold call, one good excuse is to inquire about the length requirements for submitting an op-ed piece. Many of the op-ed editors are very willing to hear your ideas over the phone and give you some indication as to whether they would be interested in such a column. If you get a welcoming response, you are sure to get a closer read from the editor. On the other hand, some op-ed editors refuse to talk with uninvited freelancers on the phone; fortunately that holds for most of your competition as well.

- *Be provocative, if not outrageous.* Staff and syndicated columnists don't need to produce gems all the time, but you do. It is particularly important to have a strong opening sentence and paragraph. (This is true in any kind of writing, of course, but in the op-ed business, it is essential in order to get read beyond this point.) One useful strategy is to turn a phrase in an interesting or ironic way as an opening line. Another is to make immediate reference to a major news event.

  Ann Thompson of the *Fort Worth Star-Telegram* emphasizes the need to grab the attention of the editor from the outset: "I can tell after reading the first two paragraphs whether this piece is worth my time—and my readers'. Keep it focused and bright. Make your point fast. And if your point is not provocative—if it repeats the conventional wisdom—forget it."

- *Be different.* You are competing against syndicated columnists who write on a regular basis about the major topics of the day. Indeed, many op-ed editors strongly advise not to duplicate what the syndicated writers are saying.

- *Be relevant.* A few newspapers definitely consider themselves to have a national audience, and therefore prefer op-ed submissions that address national or international issues. Most newspapers, however, strongly favor subject matters that have a direct bearing on local concerns. Thus if you're submitting to a local paper that is not *your* local paper, try to give the piece an angle that will appeal specifically to that local readership. "The key is a local *subject*," says Bob Ewegen of the *Denver Post*. "I'd take a Seattle writer on a Denver subject over a Denver writer musing about Nicaragua."

- *Be timely.* Most op-eds must have some "hook" (also known as a news "peg," "slant," or "angle"); that is, a strong connection to an important event in the news. This requires quick thinking and writing before interest in the issue wanes. As Tom Peeling of the *Palm Beach Post* remarked, "If you're commenting on something that happened more than 4 days ago, save it for a magazine."

  You also must consider a quick mode of delivery. Overnight delivery is fast but costly. Most newspapers accept fax transmissions of op-ed submissions, particularly if time is of the essence. Take full advantage of this technology. If you choose to fax your submission, avoid annoying the editor by later calling just to see if it arrived. As Harold Piper, op-ed editor for the *Baltimore Sun*, warned, "If you don't trust the fax, then use the mail."

- *Plan ahead.* Keep a column on your word processor until the time is right. Even if your column does not have a relationship to a current news story, one will likely come around in the not-too-distant future. It is usually a good idea to hold onto a column until it becomes newsworthy, and then simply rewrite the beginning and end to fit the news of the day. In some cases, you can even anticipate the date when your column may be newsworthy. For example, you can certainly prepare a piece to coincide with an upcoming political convention or the expected release of government statistics on unemployment trends. Also, the anniversary of a major event (e.g., the first anniversary of a devastating earthquake or the tenth anniversary of an assassination) can provide an opportunity for planning ahead.

- *Feel free to multiple submit.* This is an uncomfortable practice for most academics who are accustomed to the policies of scholarly journals that insist on exclusive submission. Most local and regional newspapers do not care if you submit the same column to other noncompeting newspapers (such as the *Philadelphia Inquirer* and the *Cleveland Plain Dealer*), although some editors appreciate being informed. Thus in order to increase your chances of acceptance, particularly in response to a fast-breaking or quick-moving story, you may submit to as many markets as you wish. You are expected, however, not to submit simultaneously to more than one newspaper in the same market (e.g., the *Chicago Tribune* and the *Chicago Sun-Times*). Should a particular newspaper decline your submission, you may, of course, then submit within the same readership market. Finally, it is critical to note that multiple submissions are not permitted by newspapers that consider themselves national publications, such as *The New York Times*, the *Los Angeles Times*, the *Washington Post*, *USA Today*, and the *Christian Science Monitor*.

- *Feel free to multiple publish.* If you are lucky enough that two or more papers in noncompeting markets accept your submission, you need not choose one over the others. Not only does this widen your audience, but the multiple checks are nice as well. Academics find the notion of multiple publication even more improper than multiple submission. Unlike scholarly journals, however, most local and regional newspapers do not take transfer of copyright when you publish a column with them. Thus you are permitted to publish the same piece (modified if necessary to fit the local context) in as many newspapers with nonoverlapping markets as you choose.

- *Make sure you understand an offer to have your column reprinted by a news service.* Hundreds of local newspapers, large and small, participate in various national news services or syndicates (e.g., the New York Times News Service or the Los Angeles Times Syndicate). After publishing a piece in a member newspaper, the op-ed editor may solicit your willingness to submit the column for syndication. This can result in dozens of other newspapers reprinting your column and thus can significantly widen the audience. At the same time syndication will also prohibit you from multiple-submission/publication on your own. Unless you are interested in doing the leg work needed to publish your column in a number of papers, however, syndication is recommended (even though you will not reap any additional financial benefits from it).

- *Recycle your material.* Dusting off your column about Passover every year is perfectly kosher. Should your story have a recurrent hook (such as a column tied to the opening of the school year or to a holiday such as Memorial Day), you may choose to reuse it for a new set of newspapers every year. Syndicated columnists often do this as well.

Case Study

During the 1988 presidential campaign, the issue of crime became a deciding concern for many voters around the country. Dukakis's stand on the death penalty, in particular, was a major stumbling block for him during the second Bush-Dukakis debate. Because of the urgency and timeliness of the topic, we simultaneously submitted (by fax) to four newspapers a column that was critical of the overemphasis on crime in the presidential campaign. This was the first time we tried a multiple submission and decided to worry later about a possible "embarrassment of riches." As it turned out, two large midwestern papers (the *Chicago Tribune* and the *Detroit Free Press*) accepted our submission. We called the op-ed editors of both papers to alert them to what we thought would be a conflict—

that another newspaper had accepted the column as well. We learned instead that the *Chicago Tribune* only cared if the other paper were the *Chicago Sun,* and the *Detroit Free Press* only minded if we were also dealing with the *Detroit News.* We were shocked, happy, and gladly cashed both checks.

In Our Opinion

Having been involved in all forms of mass media, both electronic and print, we can safely say that publishing op-ed columns has been the most rewarding. For one thing, writing on the opinion page has the potential for reaching and influencing key decision makers. Moreover, as writers, we appreciate the opportunity to craft in our words a well-reasoned argument about something that is important to us. The amount of control over the product far exceeds that of any other medium.

Q&A With
Rachelle Cohen
Editorial Page Editor,
The Boston Herald

Q. What do you see as your primary objective?

A. My primary objective is to add another dimension to what appears on our news pages. What I am looking for is something that is going to spin off of those things "in the front of the book," as we call it—things that either anticipate events that are going to be happening in the reasonably near future or respond to things that have been in the news. We allow ourselves the occasional luxury of a humor piece or a life-style piece. But for the most part, especially when it comes to those things that academics would be writing about, we are looking for pieces that add depth, perception, and analysis.

Q Would you describe the process after you receive a submission?

A. Occasionally, even before receiving a submission, a prospective contributor will call up. Query letters are, quite frankly, an absolute pain. They waste the writer's time; they waste my time. By the time there is an exchange of views, frequently the topic has come and gone. However, a phone call is frequently useful. First, it lets me know that someone out there is interested in writing on a particular topic, and, second, it allows me to communicate what I am looking for in terms of length and time frame.

Q. Do you ever solicit op-ed columns?

A. Yes, especially if we have the luxury of doing that in advance—for example, if I know there is an important Supreme Court decision coming down the road, and we know its approximate date. Probably no more than 10% to 20% of our columns are solicited from writers. It is more the exception than the rule. It has to be a very big event, and one that we will probably anticipate. More often than not, I deal with people who call and say, "I would like to write on topic X. Are you interested?" Then, if indeed I am interested in the topic, I want to know where the writer stands in terms of point of view. If I'm looking for balance, I do not want pieces coming in from two or three people on the same side of the issue.

An initial phone call will also allow me to plan. I may already have two or three pieces on my desk that I like and that I am just trying to find room for on the same topic. In this case, I might say, "It's a swell idea, but I'm already up to my eyeballs in pieces on Somalia." Then, once the piece is in hand, it is a matter of placement. Word requirements are fairly important for us. Our pieces run anywhere from 600 to 1,200 words. Writers should know this ahead of time. I don't like to cut pieces, especially pieces written by academics, because they know what is not important to them. What is important to them may not be what is important to me, and you don't want to set up that kind of conflict ahead of time. If a piece comes in at the right length, it makes everybody's job a lot easier.

Q. How long does it usually take before a column actually runs?

A. A lot depends on the topic. I very rarely accept a piece that I'm not going to use within the following 2 weeks— unless it's a holiday piece that comes to me well in advance or it's more of a life-style piece.

Q. Are there particular topics that you prefer?

A. My pages run heavily toward politics, economics, and a little bit of foreign policy. But I'm more inclined toward state and local politics, if I can get it. I consider the community that our newspaper serves. We have a tremendous wealth of resources, all those universities right outside my window. So, if I get a call from Podunk U. in the Ozarks, I am not favorably inclined to go outside our immediate circulation area. There may be editors who don't have the kinds of resources I do, who might be more favorably inclined. But I don't have to go very far. And I think people identify not only with the topic, but also with the writer, which makes it important for the writer to be "in their own backyard." That's almost an entry-level requirement for me.

Q. Do you have any advice for academics interested in contributing op-ed columns?

A. Read, read, and read. If you want to submit a piece to the *Boston Herald*, what you ought to be doing is reading the *Boston Herald* over the span of at least a couple of weeks. That gives writers a good indication of the topics and length we prefer. And it certainly saves a lot of my time— what I am looking for is in the paper every day. All someone with a reasonable brain needs to do is to look at a variety of those pages, and they'll know in fairly short order exactly the kinds of pieces that will be successful in being placed.

Table 6.1 Op-Ed Survey

Newspaper/ Op-Ed Editor	Address	Phone/Fax	Accept/ Local Preferred	Circulation/ Geographic Rights	Length/ Payment
Albany Times Union Joann Crupi	Box 15000, News Plaza Albany, NY 12212	(518) 454-5470 (518) 454-5514	Occasionally Local preferred	170K Albany area	800 $50
Arizona Daily Star Susan Albright	P.O. Box 26807 Tucson, AZ 85726	(602) 573-4233 (602) 573-4141	Occasionally Local preferred	100K (D)/170K (S) Arizona	800 max $35–$50+
Arizona Republic Stephanie Hudson	P.O. Box 1950 Phoenix, AZ 85001	(602) 271-8292 (602) 271-8933	Occasionally Local preferred	360K (D)/600K (S) Phoenix area	700 $50+
Arkansas Democrat Meredith L. Oakley	Capital Avenue & Scott Street P.O. Box 2221 Little Rock, AR 72203	(501) 378-3481 (501) 372-3908	Occasionally Local only	200K+ Arkansas	500–750 None
Atlanta Journal Peter Kent	P.O. Box 4689 Atlanta, GA 30302	(404) 526-5311 (404) 526-5610	Regularly Local preferred	175K Georgia	600 max None
Atlanta Journal Constitution Susan Stevenson	72 Marietta Street NW Atlanta, GA 30303	(404) 526-5432 (404) 526-5611	Regularly Local preferred	300K (D)/650K (S) Georgia, Alabama, Carolinas	600–700 $75–$250
Baltimore Sun Harold Piper	501 North Calvert Street Baltimore, MD 21278	(410) 332-6053 (410) 752-6049	Regularly Local preferred	240K Mid-Atlantic	500–1500 $100
Bergen County Record Roy Graham	150 River Street Hackensack, NJ 07024	(201) 646-4239 (201) 646-4135	Occasionally Local preferred	165K (D) Central/Northern New Jersey	800–1000 $50–$75
Boston Globe Marjorie Pritchard	P.O. Box 2378 Boston, MA 02107	(617) 929-3041 (617) 929-2098	Occasionally No preference	500K(D)/750K (S) New England	up to 700 $100

Publication / Contact	Address	Phone	Frequency	Circulation / Area	Length / Pay
Boston Herald Rachelle G. Cohen	1 Herald Square Boston, MA 02106-2096	(617) 426-3000 (617) 542-1315	Occasionally Local preferred	366K Massachusetts, Rhode Island, New Hampshire	600-800 $75-$100
Buffalo News Foster Spencer	1 News Plaza Box 100 Buffalo, NY 14240	(716) 849-3445 (716) 856-5150	Occasionally Local preferred	325K Buffalo	600-800 $40
Charlotte Observer Jane McAlister Pope	600 South Tryon Street P.O. Box 32188-28232 Charlotte, NC 28202	(704) 358-5017 (704) 358-5022	Regularly Local only	300K Carolinas	750 $50
Chicago Sun-Times Thomas Frisbie	401 North Wabash Avenue Chicago, IL 60611	(312) 321-2516 (312) 321-3084	Regularly Local only	530K Chicago area	600 $0
Chicago Tribune Ruby Scott	435 North Michigan Avenue Chicago, IL 60611	(312) 222-4594 (312) 222-3143	Regularly No preference	733K(D)/1.1M (S) Midwest	600-1,000 $75-$100
Christian Science Monitor Keith Henderson	1 Norway Street Boston, MA 02115	(617) 450-2370 (617) 450-2317	Regularly No preference	120K Worldwide	700-900 $100
Cincinnati Enquirer Peter Bronson	312 Elm Street Cincinnati, OH 45202	(513) 768-8301 (513) 768-8610	Occasionally Local preferred	250K (D)/300K (S) None	750 None
Cincinnati Post Robert White	125 East Court Street Cincinnati, OH 45202	(513) 352-2000 (513) 621-3962	Occasionally Local preferred	100K Cincinnati area	800-850 $50
Cleveland Plain Dealer Jim Strang	1801 Superior Avenue NE Cleveland, OH 44114	(216) 344-4146 (216) 694-6370	Regularly No preference	416K (D)/530K (S) Northeast Ohio	700-900 $50
Columbus Dispatch Mark Fisher	34 South Third Street Columbus, OH 43216	(614) 461-5067 (614) 461-7571	Occasionally Local preferred	250K (D)/400K (S) Central Ohio	500-800 $0-$50
Dallas Morning News Carolyn Barta	508 Young Street P.O. Box 65537 Dallas, TX 75265	(214) 977-8494 (214) 263-0456	Occasionally Local preferred	500K (D)/800K (S) North Texas	750 $75

Newspaper/ Op-Ed Editor	Address	Phone/Fax	Accept/ Local Preferred	Circulation/ Geographic Rights	Length/ Payment
Denver Post Bob Ewegen	P.O. Box 1709 Denver, CO 80201	(303) 820-1221 (303) 820-1369	Occasionally Local only	400,000 None	700 None
Denver Rocky Mountain News Gene Torkelson	400 W. Colfax Avenue Denver, CO 80232	(303) 892-5055 (303) 892-5123	Occasionally Local preferred	380K (D)/430K (S) Mountain region	600-700 None
Detroit Free Press Bill Rapai	321 West Lafayette Blvd. Detroit, MI 48231	(313) 222-6704 (313) 222-6774	Occasionally Local preferred	600K Michigan and Northwest Ohio	800 $50-$250
Detroit News Anne Abate	615 West Lafayette Blvd. Detroit, MI 48231	(313) 222-2297 (313) 222-6417	Regularly Local preferred	420K Michigan	up to 850 $75
Florida Times-Union Billee Bussard	P.O. Box 1949 Jacksonville, FL 32231	(904) 359-4104 (904) 359-4478	Occasionally Local preferred	200K Jacksonville area	up to 750 None
Fort Worth Star-Telegram Ann Thompson	400 West 7th Street P.O. Box 1870 Fort Worth, TX 76101	(817) 390-7752 (817) 390-7789	Occasionally Local preferred	250K (D)/343K (S) North Central Texas	800-1,000 $75
Fresno Bee Tom Kirwan	1626 E Street Fresno, CA 93786	(209) 441-6385 (209) 441-6436	Occasionally Local preferred	160K San Joaquin Valley	800 $100
Houston Chronicle Frank Michel	P.O. Box 4260 Houston, TX 77210	(713) 220-7077 (713) 220-6575	Regularly Local preferred	600K Houston area	800-900 None
Houston Post Fred King	P.O. Box 4747 Houston, TX 77210-4747	(713) 840-5823 (713) 840-6722	Regularly Local preferred	300K (D)/400K (S) Southeast Texas	900 $40
Indianapolis News Russ Pulliam	307 North Pennsylvania Street Indianapolis, IN 46206	(317) 633-9121 (317) 630-9549	Occasionally Local preferred	90K Central	750 Indiana

Publication / Contact	Address	Phone	Frequency	Preference	Circulation	Coverage	Words	Payment
Indianapolis Star John H. Lyst	307 North Pennsylvania Street Box 145 Indianapolis, IN 46206-0145	(317) 633-9170 (317) 633-9423	Occasionally	Local preferred	227K (D)/410K (S)	Indiana	600-900	$40
Kansas City Star Virginia Hall	1729 Grand Avenue Kansas City, MO 64108	(816) 234-4385 (816) 234-4926	Occasionally	Local preferred	300K	Kansas and Missouri	800	$200-$300
Las Vegas Sun Larry Wills	800 South Valley View Las Vegas, NV 89107	(702) 259-4070 (702) 383-7264	Occasionally	Local preferred	38K	Southern Nevada	750 max	$50
Los Angeles Times Bob Berger	Times Mirror Square Los Angeles, CA 90053	(213) 237-7930 (213) 237-7968	Regularly	No preference	1.2M (D)/1.5M (S)	United States	750	$150-$250
Louisville Courier-Journal Keith Runyon/ Ed Bennett	525 West Broadway Louisville, KY 40202	(502) 582-4615 (502) 582-4075	Regularly	Local only	250K	Louisville area	750-1,000	$50
Miami Herald Jim Hampton	1 Herald Plaza Miami, FL 33132-1693	(305) 376-3518 (305) 376-8950	Occasionally	No preference	495K	South Florida	750-950	$35-$200
Milwaukee Journal James Cattey	333 West State Street P.O. Box 661 Milwaukee, WI 53201	(414) 224-2012 (414) 224-2047	Regularly	Local preferred	250K (D)/500K (S)		600	$50
Milwaukee Sentinel Ernst-Ulrich Framzen	P.O. Box 371 Milwaukee, WI 53201	(414) 224-2194 (414) 224-2049	Occasionally	Local preferred	170K	Wisconsin	1000	$50
Minneapolis Star Tribune Eric Ringham	425 Portland Avenue Minneapolis, MN 55488	(612) 673-4392 (612) 673-4359	Regularly	Local preferred	420K (D)/620K (S)	Minnesota	800	$100
New Orleans Times-Picayune Malcolm Forsyth	3800 Howard Avenue New Orleans, LA 70140	(504) 826-3434 (504) 826-3369	Occasionally	Local only	260K (D)/300K (S)	Southern Louisiana, Southern	750-800	None

Newspaper/ Op-Ed Editor	Address	Phone/Fax	Accept/ Local Preferred	Circulation/ Geographic Rights	Length/ Payment
New York Daily News Rotates weekly	220 East 42nd Street New York, NY 10017	(212) 210-1618 (212) 949-2036	Occasionally Local preferred	800K New York City and Long Island	625-675 $100
The New York Times Mitchell Levitas	229 West 43rd Street New York, NY 10036	(212) 556-1831 (withheld)	Regularly No preference	1.2 M (D)/ 1.8 M (S) United States	700 $150
Oklahoman Patrick McGuigan	P.O. Box 25125 Oklahoma City, OK 73125	(405) 475-3466 (405) 475-3971	Occasionally No preference	250K (D)/350K (S) Oklahoma	550-1,000 $0-$50
Omaha World-Herald Frank Partsch	14th & Dodge Street Omaha, NE 68102	(402) 444-1000 (402) 345-4547	Regularly Local preferred	220K Nebraska and Iowa	750 None
Oregonian Glenn Davis	1320 S.W. Broadway Portland, OR 97201	(503) 221-8174 (503) 294-4193	Regularly Local preferred	350K Pacific Northwest	1,000 $100-$125
Orlando Sentinel Michael Murphy	633 North Orange Avenue Orlando, FL 32801	(407) 420-5168 (407) 420-5286	Occasionally No preference	300K (D) Florida	700 max $50
Palm Beach Post Tom Peeling	2751 South Dixie Highway West Palm Beach, FL 33405	(407) 820-4450 (407) 820-4728	Occasionally / Seldom Local preferred	220K South Florida	700 None
Philadelphia Daily News Richard Aregood	400 North Broad Street P.O. Box 7788 Philadelphia, PA 19101	(215) 854-5912 (215) 854-5691	Seldom Local preferred	200K Philadelphia	500-600 $200-$300
Philadelphia Inquirer Philip Joyce	P.O. Box 8263 Philadelphia, PA 19101	(215) 854-4540 (215) 854-5884	Regularly Local preferred	500K (D)/1M (S) Mid-Atlantic	750 $100
Phoenix Gazette John Mark	120 E. Van Guren Phoenix, AZ 85004	(602) 271-8470 (602) 271-8933	Occasionally No preference	100K Metro Phoenix	750 $15-$20

Publication / Contact	Address	Phone	Freelance	Circulation / Area	Word count / Pay
Pittsburgh Press Isadore Shrensky	34 Boulevard of the Allies Box 566 Pittsburgh, PA 15230	(412) 263-1523 (412) 263-2014	Occasionally/ Seldom Local preferred	230K (D) / 550K (S) Western Pennsylvania	700-800 None
Providence Journal-Bulletin Robert B. Whitcomb	75 Fountain Street Providence, RI 02902-9985	(401) 277-7440 (401) 277-7439	Regularly No preference	200K (D)/275K (S) Southeastern New England	800 $75
Richmond Times-Dispatch Robert Holland	333 East Grace Street Box 85333 Richmond, VA 23293-0001	(804) 649-6306 (804) 775-8090	Occasionally Local preferred	200K None	750 None
Rochester Democrat and Chronicle James Leunk	55 Exchange Blvd. Rochester, NY 14614-2001	(716) 258-2416 (716) 258-2487	Regularly Local preferred State	130K Central and Western New York	800 $0-$75
Rochester Times-Union Douglas J. Sherman	55 Exchange Blvd. Rochester, NY 14614-2001	(716) 258-2485 (716) 258-2487	Regularly Local preferred	85K None	750 $50-$75
Sacramento Bee William Kahrl	2100 Q Street P.O Box 15779 Sacramento, CA 95852	(916) 321-1909 (916) 321-1996	Regularly Local preferred	230K Sacramento area	750 $150
Salt Lake Tribune Diane Cole	143 South Main Street P.O. Box 867 Salt Lake City, UT 84110	(801) 237-2020 (801) 521-9418	Occasionally Local preferred	115K Salt Lake City	500-800 None
San Antonio Express-News Sterlin Holmesly	P. O. Box 2171 San Antonio, TX 78297	(512) 225-7411 (512) 225-5268	Occasionally Local preferred	190K (D)/280K (S) South Texas	700 None
San Antonio Light Mark Lewis	420 Broadway P.O. Box 161 San Antonio, TX 78291	(512) 271-2700 (512) 271-2770	Occasionally Local preferred	160K (D)/225K (S) San Antonio area	700-800 None

Newspaper/ Op-Ed Editor	Address	Phone/Fax	Accept/ Local Preferred	Circulation/ Geographic Rights	Length/ Payment
San Francisco Chronicle Marsha VandeBerg	901 Mission Street #24 San Francisco, CA 94103	(415) 777-6023 (415) 512-8196	Regularly No preference	600K US/1st chance/ same day	450-650 Up to $150
San Francisco Examiner	110 Fifth Street San Francisco, CA 94121	(415) 777-7923 (415) 512-1264	Regularly No preference	150K San Francisco Bay area	700 $75
San Jose Mercury News Jim Brawley	750 Ridder Park Drive San Jose, CA 95190	(408) 920-5475 (408) 288-8060	Occasionally Local preferred	250K Northern California	800 $50
St. Louis Post-Dispatch Donna Korando	900 North Tucker Blvd. Saint Louis, MO 63101	(314) 340-8391 (314) 340-3139	Regularly Local preferred	390K (D) 100 mile radius	750 $70
St. Paul Pioneer Press Dispatch Ronald D. Clark	345 Cedar Street Saint Paul, MN 55101-1057	(612) 228-5500 (612) 228-5564	Occasionally Local preferred	210K Twin Cities area	up to 750 $50
St. Petersburg Times Philip Gailey	P.O. Box 1121 Saint Petersburg, FL 33731	(813) 893-8268 (813) 893-8675	Occasionally No preference	350K (D)/450K (S) Tampa Bay area	800 $150-$200
Syracuse Post Standard Tom Boll	Box 4818 Syracuse, NY 13221	(315) 470-6045 (315) 470-3081	Occasionally Local preferred	90K Upstate New York	up to 1,000 $25
Tucson Citizen John Lankford	4850 S. Park Avenue P.O. Box 26767 Tucson, AZ 85726	(602) 573-4662 (602) 573-4569	Regularly Local preferred	55K Tucson/Pima County	650-900 None
Tulsa World Judy Randle	P.O. Box 1770 Tulsa, OK 74114	(918) 581-8331 (918) 581-8363	Rarely Local preferred	130K (D)/250K (S) Eastern Oklahoma, Western Arkansas	750 None
Wall Street Journal Amity Shloes	200 Liberty New York, NY 12281	(212) 416-2561 (212) 416-2658	Occasionally No preference	100K Worldwide	850-1100 Varies

Washington Post	1150 15th Street NW	(202) 338-7473	Regularly	800K	700
Meg Greenfield	Washington, DC 20071	(202) 338-1008	No preference	United States	$200
Washington Times	3600 New York Avenue NE	(202) 636-3000	Regularly	125K	800-1200
Mary Lou Forbes	Washington, DC 20002	(202) 529-2471	No preference	United States	$150

7 | Reasonable Expectations

We started this guidebook by outlining a variety of advantages and disadvantages associated with mass media involvement. On the one hand, media exposure increases the potential impact of your work, not to mention providing a number of more immediate fringe benefits. On the other hand, the costs of seeking publicity in terms of both the investment of time and the possible loss of credibility among colleagues cannot be ignored. Throughout this guide, we have tried to offer advice pertaining to a range of venues for enhancing the experience of working with electronic and print media. We firmly believe that, on balance, the benefits can greatly outweigh the costs, particularly if you approach the mass media in an informed way.

Similar to other academics who frequently work with the media, we have had the occasional displeasure of confronting some extremely rude, manipulative, even selfish individuals in the media who have a rather one-sided attitude. From their point of view, you are lucky that they called you and they owe you nothing. Of course, you find a few such disagreeable types in any profession, including academia for that matter. Fortunately, unpleasant media-related experiences are not the norm.

In fact, we have had the pleasure of associating, over the years, with many intelligent, socially conscious, and considerate reporters, producers, and on-air talent. Recognizing that academics donate their time to help them to do the job for which they get paid, these media representatives often go to great lengths to treat their expert sources and guests with respect. But even the best-intentioned people can get caught up in the pressure of a deadline and fail to consider the interests of others.

Therefore, when dealing with reporters and producers—the good, the bad, and the busy, it is not inappropriate in the least for the academic to be assertive about those small but important concessions that will make the media experience a positive one. Throughout the book, we have tried to give advice in order to minimize the risk of media exploitation. Actually, the academic can benefit from keeping in mind a few reasonable expectations concerning his or her treatment at the hands of the media:

- *You should make an effort to determine how you will be identified.* A producer might say that your university affiliation is irrelevant or too complicated for the audience and will instead want to identify you in a generic way. Or a newspaper reporter might mention that you wrote a book but, because of space limitations, will fail to give its title. Although there is no guarantee that the reporter will listen, care, or remember, you have a right to be firm about this vital concern.

- *You can insist that your collaborators be identified by name.* For coauthored books and articles, the ideas often belong to more than one person. It is only ethical that everyone responsible for an idea or a research finding be given credit, even if it takes up space or time. So long as you ask, you will have no reason to apologize to your colleagues.

- *You can ask the purpose of a telephone query—whether you are being contacted for research purposes only.* Imagine a student or professor whom you have never met calling you and saying, "Please tell me everything you know about your life's work. Someday, I may want to write an article that cites you, but I'm not sure yet." At times, a media researcher or reporter will do essentially the same thing. He or she will explore the possibility of doing a show or story by calling academics just to "pick" their brains. Hoping to be publicized, many academics will do for an anonymous intern or reporter over the phone what they would find objectionable to do for a student or colleague. Thus if you begin to feel that a reporter is simply pumping you for information, you should ask what their intentions are. We're not suggesting that you should refuse to be helpful; just don't be disappointed.

- *You can ask for a modest "kill fee" when a show is canceled or an article is scrubbed.* It is extremely disappointing when you learn, after telling all your friends and family, that a show you had taped has been canceled by the producer (as opposed to being preempted by a news bulletin). It is similarly frustrating to spend hours with a reporter only to find that based on an arbitrary editorial decision the story has been dropped. If a cancellation occurs under such conditions—after investing as much as a day of your valuable time in doing an interview, you can reasonably request to be compensated. You may even get it.

- *You can ask to be informed well in advance as to when you will appear on air or in print.* Reporters and producers often are unsure or change their minds regarding the exact date of a story or show. You should not be expected to scan the newspaper on a daily basis or read *TV Guide* in order to know when your interview will appear. Even if you asked to be alerted, don't assume that you will be notified. You can always make a phone call to check on scheduling.

- *You can ask reporters and producers to supply tear sheets and tapes free of charge.* For situations in which you are quoted briefly in the press or electronic media, you should not expect anything more than advance notice so that you can arrange for a copy to be made. For extensive quotes or lengthy appearances, however, the members of the media are often willing to provide copies of an article or a show—but only if you ask.

The Norm of Reciprocity

Some academics enter a media opportunity feeling that the media are omnipotent and believing that they are just lucky to get their 15 seconds of fame. Some will go to extraordinary lengths, spending time and money, in order to get on television or be featured in the press. In doing so, they run the risk of being willing victims of exploitation out of fear that, if they don't comply, someone else will be called instead. Academics who hold this mindset are particularly vulnerable—they will give a lot and expect little in return.

Other academics, in contrast, believe that they are intellectually superior to the *mass* media. They may "lower themselves" to contribute a few pearls of wisdom, but their obvious arrogance will likely assure that they will never be called again.

The best results usually occur when academics perceive a balance of power—that is, when members of the media are regarded as having equal status as professionals, though their expertise is in another line of work. Thus the norm of reciprocity applies: There are professional courtesies that you should give and professional courtesies that you should expect. For the sake of a healthy and beneficial media involvement in the long run, it is important that, whenever possible, academics ask for the small concessions we have proposed.

About the Authors/Media Bios

James Alan Fox is Professor and Dean of the College of Criminal Justice at Northeastern University in Boston. He has published eight books, including *Mass Murder: America's Growing Menace* and *Randomized Response: A Method for Sensitive Surveys*, and more than 30 articles and 20 newspaper columns, primarily in the areas of criminal statistics and multiple murder. Also, he is the founder and Editor-in-Chief of the *Journal of Quantitative Criminology*. As an authority on homicide, he appears regularly on television and radio programs around the country and is often interviewed by the press. Finally, he frequently gives lectures and expert testimony, including three appearances before the U.S. Congress.

Jack Levin is Professor of Sociology and Criminology at Northeastern University in Boston. He has authored or co-authored 16 books, including *Hate Crimes: The Rising Tide of Bigotry and Bloodshed*, *The Functions of Discrimination and Prejudice*, *Sociological Snapshots*, and *Mass Murder: America's Growing Menace*. He has published some 100 articles in professional journals such as *Criminology*, *Journal of Communication*, *The Gerontologist*, and *Youth and Society*, and newspapers and magazines around the country. As an expert on social problems such as prejudice and violence, he frequently lectures, appears on national television, and is quoted by the press. He was recently honored by the Council for Advancement and Support of Education as its Professor of the Year in Massachusetts.

JAMES ALAN FOX, Ph.D.
Professor and Dean of the College of Criminal Justice

Address: Northeastern University, Boston, Massachusetts 02115; 617-373-3296 (office), 617-373-8723 (fax), 617-555-5555 (home)

Specialties: Multiple Murder, Violence, and Capital Punishment

Publications: Eight books, including *Mass Murder: America's Growing Menace* (Plenum, Berkley paperback), *The Gainesville Student Murders* (Avon, forthcoming), and *Overkill* (Plenum, forthcoming); Thirty articles in professional journals and popular magazines, including *Boston Magazine*, *The Sunday Boston Herald Magazine* (cover story), *USA Today Magazine*, and *Celebrity Plus*. Two dozen columns in newspapers nationwide, including *Christian Science Monitor*, *USA Today*, *Boston Globe*, *Chicago Tribune*, *Detroit Free Press*, *Newsday*, *Boston Herald*, *Cleveland Plain Dealer*, *San Diego Union*, *Tampa Tribune*, *Orlando Sentinel*, and *Palm Beach Post*.

Television: Guest on national shows, including *48 Hours*, *Face the Nation*, *CBS This Morning*, *West 57th St.*, *Nightwatch*, *CBS Evening News*, *Good Morning America*, *20/20*, *ABC World News Tonight*, *Today Show*, *Faith Daniels Show*, *Unsolved Mysteries*, *NBC Nightly News*, *Larry King*, *A Current Affair*, *Geraldo*, *Oprah*, *Donahue*, *Sally Jessy Raphael*, *Maury Povich*, *Hour Magazine*, *Inside Edition*, *Hard Copy* and *Sonya*; on dozens of local programs across the country.

Radio: Hundreds of radio interviews coast-to-coast and overseas, including several network shows. Co-hosted weekly talk show on WBUR-FM (Boston).

Print Media: Quoted in thousands of news articles and magazines worldwide, including "Quote of the Day" in *The New York Times*, and "Quote of the Week" in *Newsweek*, *The Boston Globe*, and *The Seattle Times*, and Q&As in *USA Today*, *The Boston Globe* and the *Tampa Tribune*. Profiled (cover story) in *The Boston Phoenix*.

Expert Testimony: Testimony given in several trials and hearings, including three appearances before Congress.

Speaking: Dozens of major presentations nationwide at college campuses and to community and professional audiences. Represented by Wolfman Productions (New York).

JACK LEVIN, Ph.D.
Professor of Sociology and Criminology

Address: Northeastern University, Boston, Massachusetts 02115; 617-373-4983 (office), 617-373-2688 (fax), 617-555-5555 (home)

Specialties: Multiple Murder, Prejudice, Violence, and Gossip

Publications: Sixteen books, including *Mass Murder: America's Growing Menace* (Plenum, Berkley paperback); *Gossip: The Inside Scoop* (Plenum); *Hate Crimes: The Rising Tide of Bigotry and Bloodshed* (Plenum); *Ageism: Prejudice and Discrimination Against the Elderly* (Wadsworth); *Overkill* (Plenum, forthcoming); and *The Gainesville Student Murders* (Avon, forthcoming). More than one hundred articles and columns in professional journals, newspapers, and popular magazines including *Criminology, The Journal of Communication, Sex Roles, The Gerontologist, The New York Times, USA Today, The Boston Globe, The Chicago Tribune, The Detroit Free Press, The Boston Herald, The Orlando Sentinel,* and *The Palm Beach Post.* Regular columnist, *Bostonia Magazine* (1988-92).

Television: Guest on national programs, including *48 Hours, CBS This Morning, ABC Morning News, CBS Evening News, CBS Morning News, Good Morning America, Unsolved Mysteries, NBC Nightly News, Larry King, Chilean National Television, London Weekend Television, Geraldo, Oprah, Donahue, Sally Jessy Raphael, Montel Williams, Joan Rivers, Inside Edition, Now It Can Be Told,* and *Jane Whitney;* on dozens of local programs across the country.

Radio: Hundreds of radio interviews coast-to-coast and overseas, including several network shows. Co-hosted weekly talk show on WBUR-FM (Boston).

Print Media: Quoted in thousands of newspaper articles and magazines worldwide. *Q&A* in *People Magazine.* Profiled in *The Boston Globe, Newsday,* and *The Boston Phoenix.*

Expert Testimony: Consultant or expert witness in several trials and hearings.

Speaking: Hundreds of presentations nationwide at college campuses and to community and professional audiences. Represented by Wolfman Productions (New York).